Colossians
and Philemon

THE CROSSWAY CLASSIC COMMENTARIES

Colossians
and Philemon

by

J. B. Lightfoot

Series Editors

Alister McGrath and J. I. Packer

CROSSWAY BOOKS

A DIVISION OF GOOD NEWS PUBLISHERS

WHEATON, ILLINOIS • NOTTINGHAM, ENGLAND

Colossians and Philemon

Copyright © 1997 by Watermark

Published by Crossway Books

A division of Good News Publishers

1300 Crescent Street

Wheaton, Illinois 60187

First printing, 1997

Printed in the United States of America

Library of Congress Cataloging-in-Publication Data
Lightfoot, Joseph Barber, 1828-1889.
   Colossians and Philemon / by J.B. Lightfoot.
      p.   cm. — (Crossway classic commentaries)
    ISBN 0-89107-951-3
   1. Bible. N.T. Colossians—Commentaries. 2. Bible. N.T.
  Philemon—Commentaries. I. Title. II. Series.
BS2715.3.L54 1997
227'.7077—dc21   97-19164

07	06	05	04	03	02	01	00	99	98	97
15	14	13	12	11	10	9	8	7	6	5	4	3	2	1

First British edition 1997

Production and Printing in the United States of America for

CROSSWAY BOOKS

Norton Street, Nottingham, England NG7 3HR

ISBN 1-85684-144-8

*To the Right Rev. Edward Harold Brown, D.D., Lord Bishop of Winchester,
in sincere admiration of his personal character and episcopal work
and in grateful recognition of the privileges
of a private friendship.*

Contents

Series Preface

The purpose of the Crossway Classic Commentaries is to make some of the most valuable commentaries on the books of the Bible, by some of the greatest Bible teachers and theologians in the last five hundred years, available to a new generation. These books will help today's readers learn truth, wisdom, and devotion from such authors as J. C. Ryle, Martin Luther, John Calvin, J. B. Lightfoot, John Owen, Charles Spurgeon, Charles Hodge, and Matthew Henry.

We do not apologize for the age of some of the items chosen. In the realm of practical exposition promoting godliness, the old is often better than the new. Spiritual vision and authority, based on an accurate handling of the biblical text, are the qualities that have been primarily sought in deciding what to include.

So far as is possible, everything is tailored to the needs and enrichment of thoughtful readers—lay Christians, students, and those in the ministry. The originals, some of which were written at a high technical level, have been abridged as needed, simplified stylistically, and unburdened of foreign words. However, the intention of this series is never to change any thoughts of the original authors, but to faithfully convey them in an understandable fashion.

The publishers are grateful to Dr. Alister McGrath of Wycliffe Hall, Oxford, Dr. J. I. Packer of Regent College, Vancouver, and Watermark of Norfolk, England, for the work of selecting and editing that now brings this project to fruition.

THE PUBLISHERS
Crossway Books
Wheaton, Illinois

Introduction

Joseph Barbour Lightfoot (1828-1889) is widely regarded as one of the finest nineteenth-century interpreters of Paul. Lightfoot was educated at King Edward's School in Birmingham and went to the University of Cambridge in 1847. He was elected a fellow of Trinity College in 1882. Lightfoot soon developed an interest in the history, language, and culture of the New Testament period. He was one of the founders of the *Journal of Classical and Sacred Philology*. In 1861 he was appointed Hulsean Professor of Divinity at Cambridge University; in 1875 he was elected to the more senior Lady Margaret Professorship of Divinity at the same university. After only four years in this position, he was appointed Bishop of Durham and spent the remainder of his life in this position.

Lightfoot gave what were by all accounts a splendid series of lectures on the letters of Paul at Cambridge University. These lectures would form the basis of his commentaries on some of Paul's letters, many of which retain respect today. The first major commentary to be published dealt with Paul's letter to the Galatians (1865). This was followed by the commentary on Philippians (1868; already published in the Crossway Classic Commentaries series), which showed a deep love of Paul's thought and writings. His commentary on Colossians perhaps shows Lightfoot's great interest in the history and culture of the New Testament period at its best. The work dates from 1875 and shows Lightfoot's love and understanding of Paul at its most mature. Lightfoot coupled his exposition of Colossians with a brief commentary on the briefest of all of Paul's letters—Philemon.

So what can the reader expect to find in this commentary? One of its most distinctive features is obvious from the opening pages. Lightfoot begins his commentary by exploring the geography and history of the Lycus valley. The region is of major importance to early Christian history, and Lightfoot wishes his readers to gain a full understanding of the cities and events that took place in the region. It is against this backdrop that the letter to the Colossians is to be understood, and Lightfoot wishes his readers to read Paul with a firm understanding of the history and geography of the region. In its original form, the commentary engaged directly with the Greek text, and much trouble is taken over clarifying the meaning of some significant Greek terms used by Paul in the letter. Lightfoot is concerned to make sure that his readers understand the richness of Paul's message by exploring the full implications of some of the letter's central terms (such as *pleroma*, usually translated as "fullness").

Some may find Lightfoot's scholarly approach a little lacking in excitement and dynamism; others may find his English style somewhat difficult to follow at points. Be patient! There is enormous scholarly, spiritual, and theological wisdom packed into the pages of this commentary. It will bring new depth to your understanding of Colossians and its challenge to us today.

Dr. Alister E. McGrath
Principal, Wycliffe Hall

Preface to
the First Edition

by J. B. Lightfoot

On the completion of another volume of my commentary, I wish again to renew my thanks for the assistance received from previous labors in the same field. Such obligations must always be great; but it is not easy in a few words to apportion them fairly, and I shall not make the attempt. I have not consciously neglected any aid which might render this volume more complete; but at the same time I venture to hope that my previous commentaries have established my claim to be regarded as an independent worker, and in the present instance more especially I have found myself obliged to diverge widely from the treatment of my predecessors and to draw largely from other material than those which they have collected.

In the preface to a previous volume I expressed an intention of appending to my commentary on the Colossian epistle an essay on "Christianity and Gnosis." This intention has not been fulfilled to the letter; but the subject enters largely into the investigation of the Colossian heresy, where it receives as much attention as it seems to require. It will necessarily come under discussion again when the Pastoral Epistles are taken in hand.

The question of the genuineness of the two epistles contained in this volume has been deliberately deferred. It could not be discussed with any advantage apart from the Epistle to the Ephesians, for the three letters are inseparably bound together. Meanwhile, however, the doctrinal and historical discussions will, if I mistake not, have furnished answers to the main objections which have been urged; while the commentary will have shown how thoroughly natural the language and thoughts are, if conceived as arising out of an immediate emergency. More especially it will have been made apparent that the Epistle to the Colossians hangs together as a whole, and that the phenomena are altogether adverse to any theory of interpolation such as that recently put forward by Professor Holtzmann.

In the commentary, as well as in the introduction, it has been the chief aim to illustrate and develop the theological conception of the person of Christ, which underlies the Epistle to the Colossians. The Colossian heresy, for instance, owes its importance mainly to the fact that it throws this conception into bolder relief. To this portion of the subject, therefore, I venture to direct special attention.

I wish to express my obligations to Dr Schiller-Szinessy, of whose talmudical learning I have freely availed myself in verifying Frankel's quotations and in other ways. I should add, however, that he is not in any degree responsible for my conclusions and has not even seen what I have written.

Trinity College, Cambridge
April 30, 1875

COLOSSIANS

Introduction

1

The Churches
of the Lycus

The Situation of the Three Cities

Lying in, or overhanging, the valley of the Lycus, a tributary of the Maeander,
were three neighboring towns—Laodicea, Hierapolis, and Colosse. The river
flows, roughly speaking, from east to west; but at this point, which is some
few miles above its junction with the Maeander, its direction is more nearly
from southeast to northwest. Laodicea and Hierapolis stand face to face, being
situated respectively on the southern and northern sides of the valley, six miles
apart and within sight of each other, the river lying in the open plain between
them. The site of Colosse is a little upstream, about ten or twelve miles from
where the road between Laodicea and Hierapolis crosses the Lycus. Unlike
Laodicea and Hierapolis, which overhang the valley on opposite sides,
Colosse stands on the riverbank, the stream cutting the town in half. The three
cities lie so close to each other that it would be quite possible to visit them all
in a single day.

Their Neighborhood and Links

Thus situated, they would necessarily be in constant communication with
each other. We are not surprised therefore to find them so closely connected in the earliest ages of Christianity. It was the consequence of their
position that they owed their knowledge of the Gospel to the same evangelist, that the same phases of thought prevailed in them, and that they were
exposed to the same moral and intellectual temptations.

Physical Forces at Work

The physical features of the neighborhood are very striking. Two potent forces of nature are actively at work to change the face of the country, the one destroying old landmarks, the other creating fresh ground.

Frequent Earthquakes

On the one hand, the Lycus valley was and is especially liable to violent earthquakes. The same danger indeed extends over large areas of Asia Minor, but this district is singled out by the ancient writers, and the testimony of modern travelers confirms the statement as the chief theater of these catastrophes. Not once or twice only in the history of Laodicea do we read of such visitations laying waste the city itself or some flourishing town in the neighborhood. Though the exterior surface of the earth shows no traces of recent volcanoes, the cavernous nature of the soil and the hot springs and mephitic vapors abounding here indicate the presence of those subterranean fires which from time to time have manifested themselves in this work of destruction.

Limestone Deposits

But while the earth's crust is constantly broken up by these forces from beneath, another agency is actively employed above ground in laying a new surface. If fire has its fitful outbursts of devastation, water is only less powerful in its gradual work of reconstruction. The lateral streams which swell the waters of the Lycus are thickly impregnated with calcareous matter, which they deposit in their course. The limestone formations of this valley are among the most remarkable in the world, surpassing even the striking phenomena of Tivoli and Clermont. Ancient monuments are buried, fertile lands overlaid, riverbeds choked up and streams diverted, fantastic grottoes and cascades and archways of stone formed by this strange capricious power, at once destructive and creative, working silently and relentlessly through long ages. Fatal to vegetation, these incrustations spread like a stony shroud over the ground. Gleaming like glaciers on the hillside, they attract the eye of the traveler from twenty miles away and form a singularly striking feature in scenery of more than common beauty and impressiveness.

Produce and Goods from the District

At the same time, along with these destructive agencies, the fertility of the district was and is unusually great. Its rich pastures fed large flocks of sheep, whose fleeces were of superior quality; and the trade in dyed woolen goods was the chief source of the prosperity of these towns. For the bounty of nature was not confined to the production of the material but extended also to the preparation of the fabric. The mineral streams had chemical qualities which were highly valued by the dyer. Hence we find that all three towns with which we are concerned were famous in this trade. At Hierapolis, as at Thyatira, the guild of the dyers appears in the inscriptions as an important and influential body. Their colors vied in brilliancy with the richest scarlets and purples of the farther East. Laodicea again was famous for the color of its fleeces, probably a glossy black which was much esteemed. Here also we read of a guild of dyers. And lastly, Colosse gave its name to a peculiar dye which seems to have been some shade of purple and from which it derived a considerable revenue.

Laodicea

Its Name and History

Of these three towns Laodicea, as the most important, deserves to be considered first. Laodice was a common name among the ladies of the royal house of the Seleucidae, as Antiochus was among the princes. Hence Antiochia and Laodicea occur frequently as the designations of cities within the dominions of the Syrian kings. Laodicea on the Lycus, as it was surnamed to distinguish it from other towns so called, and more especially perhaps from its near neighbor Laodicea Catacecaumene, had borne in succession the names of Diospolis and Rhoas; but when refounded by Antiochus Theos (261-246 B.C.), it was newly designated after his wife Laodice. It is situated on the undulating hill, or group of hills, which overhangs the valley on the south, being washed on either side by the streams of the Asopus and the Caprus, tributaries of the Lycus. Behind it rise the snow-capped heights of Cadmus, the lofty mountain barrier which shuts in the south side of the main valley.

A place of no great importance at first, it made rapid strides in the last days of the republic and under the earliest Caesars and had become, two or three generations before St. Paul wrote, a popular and thriving city. Among its famous inhabitants are mentioned the names of some philosophers, sophists, and rhetoricians, men renowned in their day but forgotten or almost forgotten now. More to our purpose, as illustrating the boasted wealth and prosperity of the city, which appeared as a reproach and a stumbling block in the apostle John's eyes (see Revelation 3:17), are the facts that one of its citizens, Polemo, became a king and a father of kings, and that another, Hiero, having accumulated enormous wealth, bequeathed all his property to the people and adorned the city with expensive gifts. To the good fortune of her principal sons, as well as to the fertility of the country around, the geographer Strabo ascribes the increase and prosperity of Laodicea. The ruins of public buildings still bear testimony by their number and magnificence to the past greatness of the city.

Its Political Rank, as the Capital of a Conventus

Not less important, as throwing light on the apostolic history, is the political status of Laodicea. Asia Minor under the Romans was divided into districts, each comprising several towns and having its chief city, in which the courts were held from time to time by the proconsul or legate of the province, and where the taxes from the subordinate towns were collected. Each of these political aggregates were styled in Latin *conventus*, in Greek *dioiklesis*—a term later borrowed by the Christian church, being applied to a similar ecclesiastical aggregate, and thus naturalized in the languages of Christendom as diocese. At the head of the most important of these political dioceses, the "Cibyratic convention" or "jurisdiction" as it was called, comprising not less than twenty-five towns, stood Laodicea. Here in times past Cicero, a proconsul of Cilicia, had held court; hither at stated seasons flocked suitors, advocates, clerks, sheriffs' officers, tax-collectors, pleasure-seekers, courtiers—all those crowds whom business or leisure or policy or curiosity would draw together from a wealthy and populous district, when the representative of the laws and the majesty of Rome appeared to receive homage and to hold his assize.

To this chief city of the Cibyratic union a portion of the inscriptions probably refer when they style Laodicea the "metropolis." And in its metropolitan rank we see an explanation of the fact that to Laodicea, as to the center of the Christian diocese also, whence their letters would readily be circulated among the neighboring brotherhoods, two apostles addressed themselves in succession, the one writing from his captivity in Rome (see Colossians 4:16), the other from his exile at Patmos (see Revelation 3:14).

Its Religious Worship

On the religious worship of Laodicea very little special information exists. Its tutelary deity was Zeus, whose guardianship had been recognized in Diospolis, the older name of the city, and who, having (according to the legend) commanded its rebuilding, was commemorated on its coins with the surname Laodicenus. Occasionally he is also called Aseis, a title which perhaps reproduces a Syrian epithet of this deity, "the mighty." If this interpretation is correct, we have a link between Laodicea and the religions of the farther East—a connection far from improbable, considering that

20

Laodicea was refounded by a Syrian king and is not unlikely to have adopted some features of Syrian worship.

Hierapolis

Its Situation

On the north of the valley, opposite the sloping hills which mark the site of Laodicea, is a broad level terrace jutting out from the mountainside and overhanging the plain with almost precipitous sides. On the plateau are scattered the vast ruins of Hierapolis. The mountains on which it abuts occupy the wedge of ground between the Maeander and the Lycus; but as the Maeander above its junction with the Lycus passes through a narrow ravine, they blend, when seen from a distance, with the loftier range of the Mesogis which overhangs the right bank of the Maeander almost from its source to its embouchure and form with it the northern barrier to the view, as the Cadmus range does the southern, the broad valley stretching between. Thus Hierapolis may be said to lie over against Mesogis as Laodicea lies over against Cadmus.

Remarkable Physical Features

It is at Hierapolis that the remarkable physical features which distinguish the Lycus valley display themselves in all their glory. Over the steep cliffs which support the plateau of the city tumble cascades of pure white stone, the deposit of calcareous matter from the streams which, after crossing this upper level, are precipitated over the ledge into the plain beneath and assume the most fantastic shapes in their descent. At one time overhanging in cornices fringed with stalactites, at another hollowed out into basins or broken up with ridges, they mark the site of the city at a distance, glistening on the mountainside like foaming cataracts frozen in the fall.

But for the immediate history of St. Paul's letters the striking beauty of the scenery has no value. It is not probable that he had visited this district when the letters to the Colossians and Laodiceans were written. Were it otherwise, we can hardly suppose that, educated under widely different influences and occupied with deeper and more absorbing thoughts, he would have shared the enthusiasm which this scenery inspires in the modern traveler. Still, it will give a reality to our conceptions if we try to picture for ourselves the external features of that city which was destined before long to become the adopted home of apostles and other personal disciples of the Lord and to play a conspicuous part—second perhaps only to

Ephesus—in the history of the church during the ages immediately succeeding the apostles.

Hierapolis a Famous Watering Place

Like Laodicea, Hierapolis was at this time an important and growing city, though not like Laodicea holding metropolitan rank. Besides the trade in dyed wools which it shared in common with the neighboring towns, it had another source of wealth and prosperity peculiar to itself. The streams to which the scenery owes its remarkable features are endowed with valuable medicinal qualities, while at the same time they are so copious that the ancient city is described as full of self-made baths. An inscription, still legible among the ruins, celebrates their virtues in heroic verse, thus apostrophizing the city:

> Hail, fairest soil in all broad Asia's realm;
>   Hail, golden city, nymph divine, bedeck'd
> With flowing rills, thy jewels.

Coins from Hierapolis too are extant of various types, on which Aesculapius and Hygeia appear either singly or together. To this fashionable watering place, thus favored by nature, seekers of pleasure and seekers of health alike were drawn.

The Magnificence of Its Ruins

To the ancient magnificence of Hierapolis its extant ruins bear ample testimony. More favored than Laodicea, it has not in its immediate neighborhood any modern town or village of importance whose inhabitants have been tempted to quarry materials for their houses out of the memorials of its former greatness. Hence the whole plateau is covered with ruins, of which the extent and the good taste are equally remarkable; and of these the *palaestra* and the *thermae*, as might be expected, are among the more prominent.

Its Religious Worship

A city which combined the pursuit of health and of gaiety had fitly chosen as its patron deity Apollo, the god alike of medicine and of festivity, here worshiped especially as "Archegetes," the Founder. But more important, as illustrating the religious temper of this Phrygian city, is another fact connected with it. In Hierapolis was a spot called the Plutonium, a hot well or spring from whose narrow mouth issued a mephitic vapor immediately fatal to those who stood over the opening and inhaled the fumes. To the mutilated priests of Cybele alone (so it was believed) an immunity was given from heaven which freed them from its deadly effects. Indeed this city appears to have been a chief center of the passionate mystical devotion of ancient Phrygia. But indications are not lacking that in addition to this older worship, religious rites were borrowed also from other parts of the East, especially from Egypt. By the multitude of her temples Hierapolis established her right to the title of "the sacred city" which she bore.

The Birthplace of Epictetus

Though at this time we have no record of famous citizens at Hierapolis, such as graced the annals of Laodicea, yet a generation or two later she numbered among her sons one nobler far than the rhetoricians and sophists, the millionaires and princes, of whom her neighbor could boast. The lame slave Epictetus, the loftiest of heathen moralists, must have been growing up to manhood when the first rumors of the Gospel reached his native city. Did any chance throw him across the path of Epaphras, who first announced the glad tidings there? Did he ever meet the great apostle himself while dragging out his long captivity at Rome or when after his release he paid his long-promised visit to the Lycus valley? We should be glad to think that these two great men met together face to face—the greatest of Christians and the greatest of heathen preachers. Such a meeting would solve more than one riddle. A Christian Epictetus certainly was not. His Stoic doctrine and his Stoic morality are alike apparent; nevertheless, his language presents some strange coincidences with the apostolic writings, which would thus solicit an explanation. It must be confessed, however, that history furnishes us with no meeting between them.

Colosse

Difficulty in Determining Its Site

While the site of Laodicea and Hierapolis are clear, so that they were early identified by their ruins, the same is not the case with Colosse. Only within the present generation has the position of this once famous city been ascertained, and even now it lacks the confirmation of any inscription found *in situ* and giving the name.

Underground Channel of the Lycus

Herodotus states that in Colosse the river Lycus disappears in an underground cave, emerging again at a distance of about five stades; and this very singular landmark—the underground passage of a stream for half a mile—might be thought to have placed the site of the city beyond the reach of controversy. But this is not the case. In the immediate neighborhood of the only ruins which can possibly be identified with Colosse, no such underground channel has been discovered. But on the other hand the appearance of the river at this point suggests that at one time the narrow gorge through which it runs, as it crosses the ruins, was overarched for some distance with incrustations of travertine and that this natural bridge was broken up later by an earthquake to expose the channel of the stream. This explanation seems satisfactory. If it is rejected, we must look for the underground channel, not within the city itself, as the words of Herodotus strictly interpreted require, but at some point higher up the stream. In either case there can be little doubt that these are the ruins of Colosse.

Petrifying Stream

The fact mentioned by Pliny, that there is in this city a river which turns brick into stone, is satisfied by a side stream flowing into the Lycus from the north and laying large deposits of calcareous matter, though in this region such a phenomenon is very far from rare. The site of Colosse, then, as determined by these considerations, lies two or three miles north of the present town of Chonos, the medieval Chonae, and some twelve miles east of Laodicea. The Lycus crosses the site of the ruins, dividing the city into two parts, the necropolis standing on the right or northern bank, and the town itself on the left.

Its Ancient Greatness

Commanding the approaches to a pass in the Cadmus range, and standing on a great highway linking Eastern and Western Asia, Colosse at an early date appears as a very important place. Here the mighty host of Xerxes halted on its march against Greece; it is mentioned on this occasion as "a great city of Phrygia." Here, too, Cyrus remained seven days on his daring enterprise which terminated so fatally. The Greek captain who records the expedition speaks of it as "a populous city, prosperous and great." But after this its glory seems to wane. The political supremacy of Laodicea and the growing popularity of Hierapolis gradually drain its strength; and Strabo, writing about two generations before St. Paul, describes it as a "small town" in the district of which Laodicea was the capital. We will therefore be prepared to find that while Laodicea and Hierapolis both held important places in the early records of the church, Colosse disappears wholly from the pages of history. Its comparative insignificance is still attested by its ruins, which are few and meager, while the vast remains of temples, baths, theaters, aqueducts, gymnasia, and sepulchers, strewn across the extensive sites of its more fortunate neighbors, still bear witness to their ancient prosperity and magnificence. It is not even mentioned by Ptolemy, though his enumeration of towns includes several small places. Without doubt Colosse was the least important church to which any letter of St. Paul is addressed.

Their Political Relationship

Considered ethnologically, Laodicea, Hierapolis, and Colosse are generally thought of as belonging to Phrygia. Phrygia, however, ceased to have any political significance when it came under Roman rule. Politically speaking, these three cities belonged at this time to Asia, the proconsular province. Laodicea is addressed as an Asiatic church in the book of Revelation. To this province these cities had been assigned in the first instance; then they were handed over to Cilicia; afterwards they were transferred and transferred back from one to the other until finally, before the Christian era, they became a permanent part of Asia, their original province.

Important Jewish Settlement in Its Neighborhood

The letter to the Colossians supposes a powerful Jewish colony in Laodicea and the neighborhood. We are not, however, left to draw this inference from the letter alone, but the fact is established by ample independent testimony. When, with the insolent license characteristic of oriental kings, Antiochus the Great transported 2,000 Jewish families from Babylonia and Mesopotamia into Lydia and Phrygia, we can hardly doubt that among the principal stations of these new colonists would be the most thriving cities of Phrygia, which were also the two most important settlements of the Syrian kings Apamea and Laodicea, the one founded by his grandfather Antiochus the First, the other by his father Antiochus the Second.

Accordingly, under the Roman domination we find them gathered here in very large numbers. When Flaccus the propraetor of Asia (62 B.C.) forbade the contributions of the Jews to the temple worship and the consequent movement of the money to Palestine, he seized as contraband not less than twenty pounds weight in gold in a single district of which Laodicea was the capital. Calculated at the rate of a half-shekel for each man, this sum represents a population of more than 11,000 adult freemen, for women, children, and slaves were exempted. It will also be remembered that Phrygia is especially mentioned among those countries which furnished their quota of worshipers at Jerusalem and were thus represented at the baptism of the Christian church on the great day of Pentecost (Acts 2:10).

Special Attractions of Hierapolis

Mention has already been made of the trade in dyed wools which formed the staple commerce in the valley of the Lycus. It may be inferred from other notices that this branch of trade had a peculiar attraction for the Jews (Acts 16:14). If so, their commercial instincts would constantly bring fresh recruits to a colony which was already very considerable. But the neighborhood held out other inducements besides this. Hierapolis, the attractive watering place, the pleasant resort of the lazy, had charms for them, as well as Laodicea, the busy commercial city. At least such was the complaint of stricter patriots at home. "The wines and the baths of Phrygia," writes a Talmudist bitterly, "have separated the ten tribes from Israel."

St. Paul Had Not Visited the District When He Wrote

There is no ground for supposing that when St. Paul wrote his letter to the Colossians, he had ever visited the church in which he evinces so deep an interest. Whether we examine the narrative in the Acts of the Apostles, or whether we gather up the notices in the letter itself, we find no hint that he had ever been in this neighborhood; but on the contrary some expressions indirectly exclude the supposition of a visit to the district.

What Is Meant by Phrygia in St. Luke?

It is true that St. Luke more than once mentions Phrygia as lying on St. Paul's route or as witnessing his labors. But Phrygia was a vague and comprehensive term; nor can we assume that the valley of the Lycus was intended unless the direction of his route or the context of the narrative distinctly points to this southwestern corner of Phrygia. In neither of the two passages where St. Paul is stated to have traveled through Phrygia is this the case (Acts 16:6; 18:23). St. Luke's narrative seems to exclude any visit of the apostle to the churches of the Lycus before his first Roman captivity.

St. Luke's Narrative Borne out by St. Paul's Own Words

This inference is confirmed by St. Paul's own language to the Colossians. He represents his knowledge of their continued progress, and even of their first initiation in the truths of the Gospel, as derived from the report of others. He describes himself as having "heard" of their faith in Christ and their love for the saints (Colossians 1:4). He recalls the day when he first "heard" of their Christian profession and zeal (1:9). Though opportunities occur again and again where he would naturally have referred to his direct personal relationship with them if he had been their evangelist, he abstains from any such reference. He speaks of them being instructed in the Gospel, of his own preaching the Gospel, several times in the course of the letter, but he never links the two together, even though the one reference stands in the immediate neighborhood of the other (1:5-8, 21-23, 25, 28-29; 2:5-6).

Moreover, if he had actually visited Colosse, it must seem strange that he should not once allude to any incident occurring while he stayed there, for this letter would then be the single exception to his usual practice. And, lastly, in one passage at least, if interpreted in its natural sense, he declares that the Colossians were not known to him personally (2:1).

Epaphras Was the Evangelist of This District

But if Paul was not directly their evangelist, yet to him they were indirectly indebted for their knowledge of the truth. Epaphras had been his delegate to them, his representative in Christ. By Epaphras they had been converted to the Gospel. This is the evident meaning of a passage in the opening of the letter, 1:6-8.

St. Paul's Stay at Ephesus Instrumental in Their Conversion

How or when the conversion of the Colossians took place, we have no direct information. Yet it can hardly be wrong to connect the event with St. Paul's long stay at Ephesus. Here he remained preaching for three whole years. It is possible indeed that during this period he paid short visits to other neighboring cities of Asia; but if so, the notices in the Acts oblige us to suppose these interruptions to his stay in Ephesus were short and infrequent (20:18).

Yet, though the apostle himself was stationary in the capital, the apostle's influence and teaching spread far beyond the limits of the city and its immediate neighborhood. It was hardly an exaggeration when Demetrius declared that "this fellow Paul has convinced and led astray large numbers of people here in Ephesus and in practically the whole province of Asia" (Acts 19:26). The sacred historian himself uses equally strong language in describing the effects of the apostle's preaching: "all the Jews and Greeks who lived in the province of Asia heard the word of the Lord" (Acts 19:10).

In line with this, the apostle himself in a letter written during his stay at Ephesus sends greetings to Corinth, not from the church of Ephesus specially, as might have been anticipated, but from "the churches in the province of Asia" (1 Corinthians 16:19). Generally St. Luke, it should be observed, ascribes this dissemination of the Gospel not to journeys undertaken by the apostle, but to his preaching at Ephesus itself (Acts 19:10). To that place, as to the city of western Asia, crowds flocked from all the towns and villages near and far. From there they would carry away, each to his own neighborhood, the spiritual treasure which they had so unexpectedly found.

Relationships Between These Cities and Ephesus

Among the places thus represented at the Asiatic city would doubtless be the cities lying in the Lycus valley. The relationships between these places and Ephesus appear to have been unusually intimate. The "Concord of the Laodiceans and Ephesians," the "Concord of the Hierapolitans and Ephesians" are repeatedly commemorated on the medals struck for the purpose. Thus the Colossians, Epaphras and Philemon, the latter with his household (Philemon 1, 2, 19), and perhaps also the Laodicean Nympha (Colossians 4:15) would fall in with the apostle of the Gentiles and hear from his lips the first tidings of a heavenly life.

Especially Epaphras

But whatever service may have been rendered by Philemon at Colosse, or by Nympha at Laodicea, it was to Epaphras especially that all three cities were indebted for their knowledge of the Gospel. Though he was a Colossian by birth, the fervency of his prayers and the energy of his love are represented as extending equally to Laodicea and Hierapolis (Colossians 4:12-13). It is obvious that he looked on himself as responsible for the spiritual well-being of all alike.

St. Paul Still a Stranger to This District

We pass over a period of five or six years. St. Paul's first captivity in Rome is now drawing to a close. During this interval he has not once visited the Lycus valley. He has, it is true, skirted the coast and called at Miletus, which lies near the mouth of the Maeander; but though the elders of Ephesus were summoned to meet him there (Acts 20:16-17), no mention is made of any representatives from these more distant towns. While St. Paul was still a prisoner in Rome, friends new and old minister freely to his needs. Meanwhile, the alienation of the Judaic Christians is complete. Three only, remaining faithful to him, are commemorated as honorable exceptions in the general desertion (Colossians 4:10-11).

Colosse Brought to St. Paul's Attention for Two Reasons

We have seen that Colosse was an unimportant place and that it had no direct personal claims on the apostle. We might therefore feel surprised

28

that, thus doubly disqualified, it should nevertheless attract his special attention at a critical moment, when severe personal trials were added to his facing daily the pressure of his concern for all the churches (see 2 Corinthians 11:28). But two circumstances, the one affecting his public duties, the other private and personal, happened at this time which conspired to bring Colosse to his attention in a major way.

The Mission of Epaphras

He had received a visit from Epaphras. The dangerous condition of the Colossian and neighboring churches had filled the mind of their evangelist with alarm. A strange form of heresy had broken out in these brotherhoods—a combination of Judaic formalism and oriental mystic speculation—and was already spreading rapidly. His distress was extreme. He gratefully acknowledged and reported their faith in Christ and their works of love (Colossians 1:4, 8). But this only increased his anxiety. He had "not stopped praying" for them (Colossians 1:9) that they might stand fast and not abandon the simplicity of their earlier faith (Colossians 1:12-13). Epaphras came to Rome, we may suppose, for the express purpose of laying this state of things before the apostle and seeking his counsel and assistance.

Onesimus—A Fugitive in Rome

But at the time when Epaphras paid this visit, St. Paul was also in close touch with another Colossian, who had visited Rome under very different circumstances. Onesimus, the runaway slave, had sought the city probably as a convenient hiding-place where he might escape detection among its crowds and make a livelihood as best he could. Here, perhaps accidentally, perhaps through the intervention of Epaphras, he fell in with his master's old friend. The apostle interested himself in his case, instructed him in the Gospel, and transformed him from a good-for-nothing slave (Philemon 11) into a "faithful and dear brother" (Colossians 4:9; compare Philemon 16).

The Apostle Sends Off Three Letters Simultaneously

This combination of circumstances called the apostle's attention to the churches of the Lycus valley, and especially to Colosse. St. Paul's letters, which had been found weighty and powerful in other places, might not be unavailing now; and in this hope he took up his pen. Three letters were written and dispatched at the same time to this district.

The Letter to the Colossians

St. Paul addresses a special letter to the Colossians, written in the joint names of himself and Timothy, warning them against the errors of the false teachers. He gratefully acknowledges the report which he has received of their love and zeal (1:3-9, 21ff.). He urges them to be on their guard against the delusive logic of enticing words, against the vain deceit of a false philosophy (2:4, 8, 18).

Theological and Practical Errors. The purity of their Christianity is endangered by two errors, recommended to them by their heretical leaders—the one theological, the other practical—but both springing from the same source: the conception of matter as the origin and abode of evil. Thus, regarding God and matter as directly antagonistic and therefore apart from and having no link with each other, they tried to explain the creation and rule of the world by interposing a series of intermediate beings, emanations, or angels, to whom accordingly they offered worship. At the same time, since they held that evil resided, not in the rebellious spirit of man, but in the innate properties of matter, they sought to overcome it by a rigid ascetic discipline, which failed after all to touch the springs of action.

The Corrective to Both Lies in the Christ of the Gospel. As both errors flowed from the same source, they must be corrected by the application of the same remedy, the Christ of the Gospel. In the person of Christ, the one mediator between heaven and earth, is the true solution of the theological difficulty. Through life in Christ, the purification of the heart through faith and love, is the effectual triumph over moral evil (Colossians 1:1-20; 2:9; 3:4). St. Paul, therefore, prescribes to the Colossians the true teaching of the Gospel as the best antidote to the twofold danger which threatens at once their theological creed and their moral principles, while at the same time he enforces his lesson by the claims of personal affection, appealing to the devotion of their evangelist Epaphras on their behalf (1:7; 4:12).

Epaphras. Of Epaphras himself we know nothing beyond the few but significant notices which connect him with Colosse. He did not return to Colosse as the bearer of the letter but remained behind with St. Paul (Colossians 4:12). As St. Paul in a contemporary letter designates him his fellow-prisoner (Philemon 23), it may be inferred that Epaphras' zeal and affection had involved him in the apostle's captivity and that his stay in Rome was enforced. However this may be, the letter was placed in the hands of Tychicus, who had been born in proconsular Asia, probably in Ephesus (Acts 20:4; 2 Timothy 4:12) and who was entrusted with a wider mission at this time, which involved him in visiting the Lycus valley.

30

Tychicus and Onesimus Accompany the Letter. Tychicus was accompanied by Onesimus, whom the Colossians had only known up to that point as a worthless slave, but who now returns to them with the stamp of the apostle's warm approval. St. Paul says very little about himself because Tychicus and Onesimus would be able by word of mouth to communicate all the information to the Colossians (Colossians 4:7-9).

The Greetings. But St. Paul sends one or two greetings which deserve a few words of explanation. Epaphras, of course, greets his fellow-townsmen and children in the faith. Other names also appear (Colossians 4:10-14):

Aristarchus the Thessalonian, who had been with the apostle at Ephesus (Acts 19:29), may possibly have formed some personal link with the Colossians at that time.

Mark, against whom apparently the apostle fears that a prejudice may be entertained (perhaps the fact of his earlier desertion and St. Paul's dissatisfaction in consequence, Acts 13:13; 15:37-39, may have been widely known), and for whom therefore the apostle asks a favorable reception at this approaching visit to Colosse, according to instructions which they had already received.

Jesus the Just, whose links with the Colossians we know nothing about and whose only claim to a mention may have been his singular faithfulness to the apostle at a critical juncture.

Greetings are also added from Luke and Demas; and here again their close link with the apostle is, so far as we know, the sole reason for their names appearing.

Instructions about Laodicea. Lastly, the Laodiceans were closely linked with the Colossians by local and spiritual ties. To the church of Laodicea, therefore, and to the household of one Nympha, who was a prominent member of it, Paul sends greetings. At the same time he directs the Colossians to exchange letters with the Laodiceans, for to Laodicea also he had written. And he closes his greetings with a message to Archippus, a resident either at Colosse or at Laodicea (on this point we are left to conjecture), who held some important office in the church and about whose zeal Paul seems to have entertained a misgiving (Colossians 4:15-17).

The Letter to Philemon

While providing for the spiritual welfare of the whole Colossian church, St. Paul did not forget the temporal interests of its humblest member. Having attended to the solicitations of the evangelist Epaphras, he now addressed himself to the troubles of the runaway slave Onesimus. The mission of Tychicus to Colosse was a favorable opportunity of restoring that slave to Philemon, for Tychicus, well-known as the apostle's friend and fellow-laborer, might throw the shield of his protection over Onesimus and avert the worst consequences of Philemon's anger. But, not content with this precaution, the apostle himself writes to Philemon on the offender's behalf, recommending him as a changed man (Philemon 11, 16) and claiming forgiveness for him as a return due from Philemon to himself as to his spiritual father (Philemon 19).

The greetings in this letter are the same as those in the letter to the Colossians with the exception of Jesus Justus, whose name is omitted (Philemon 23-24). Toward the end of the letter St. Paul declares his hope of release and his intention of visiting Colosse and asks Philemon to "prepare a guest room" for him (Philemon 22).

The Circular Letter, of Which a Copy Is Sent to Laodicea

But at the same time, with the two letters destined especially for Colosse, the apostle sent a third letter which had a wider scope. It has been already mentioned that Tychicus was entrusted with a mission to the Asiatic churches. It has been noticed also that the Colossians were directed to procure and read a letter in the possession of the Laodiceans. These two facts are closely linked. The apostle wrote at this time a circular letter to the Asiatic churches, which received its ultimate designation from the metropolitan city and is consequently known to us as the letter to the Ephesians. The immediate purpose of Tychicus' journey was to deliver copies of this letter at all the principal centers of Christianity in the district, and at the same time to communicate by word of mouth the apostle's special messages to each (Ephesians 6:21-22). Among those centers was Laodicea. Thus his mission brought him into the immediate neighborhood of Colosse. But he was not told to deliver another copy of the circular letter at Colosse itself, for this church would be thought of only as a dependent of Laodicea; and besides, he was the bearer of a special letter from the apostle to them. It was sufficient, therefore, to provide that the Laodiceans' copy should be circulated and read at Colosse.

Personal Links Connecting the Three Letters

Thus the three letters are closely related. Tychicus is the personal link between the letters to the Ephesians and to the Colossians; Onesimus is the personal link between the letters to the Colossians and to Philemon.

The Chronology of These Letters

It would appear that these three letters were written and sent toward the end of the apostle's captivity, about A.D. 63. At some time not very far from this date, a great catastrophe overtook the cities of the Lycus valley. An earthquake was a common occurrence in this region. But on this occasion the shock had been unusually violent, and Laodicea, the flourishing and well-populated town, was laid in ruins. Tacitus, the Roman historian, records that Laodicea was rebuilt from her own resources without the usual assistance from Rome.

St. Mark's Intended Visit and St. Paul's Probable Visit to Colosse

When these letters were written St. Mark was intending to visit Colosse soon. Also the apostle Paul himself, looking forward to his own release, hoped to at last make a personal acquaintance with these churches, which up until then he had only known through other people's reports. Whether St. Mark's visit was ever paid or not we have no means of determining. Of St. Paul himself it is reasonable to assume that in the interval between his first and second Roman captivity he found some opportunity of making his intended visit. At all events we find him at Miletus, near the mouth of the Maeander (2 Timothy 4:20), and the journey from there to Laodicea is neither long nor difficult.

St. John in Asia Minor

At the time of this visit—the first and last, we may suppose, which he paid to the Lycus valley—St. Paul's direction of the Asiatic churches is drawing to a close. With his death they pass into the hands of St. John, who goes to live in Asia Minor. Of Colosse and Hierapolis we hear nothing more in the New Testament; but from his exile on the island of Patmos the beloved disciple delivers his Lord's message to the church of Laodicea (Revelation 3:14-22), a message doubtless intended to be given also to the two subordinate churches, to which it would apply almost equally well.

Similarities Between the Book of Revelation and St. Paul's Letters

The message given by St. John to Laodicea prolongs the note which was struck by St. Paul in the letter to Colosse. An interval of a very few years has not materially altered the character of these churches. Obviously the same mood prevails, the same errors are rife, the same correction must be applied.

Teaching About the Person of Christ. While St. Paul finds it necessary to enforce the truth that Christ is the image of the invisible God and that in him all the divine fullness dwells, and that he existed before all things, and that through him all things were created and in him all things are sustained, and that he is the primary source and has preeminence in all things (Colossians 1:15-18), so in almost identical language St. John, speaking in the person of our Lord, declares that Christ is the Amen, the faithful and true witness, the primary source of God's creation (Revelation 3:14). It should be observed that the title of our Lord, "the ruler of God's creation" (Revelation 3:14), which so closely resembles the language of the Colossian letter, does not occur in the messages to the other six churches in the book of Revelation; nor do we find there anything resembling it. Some lingering shreds of the old heresy, we may suppose, still hung around these churches, and instead of holding fast to the Head, they were still prone to substitute intermediate agencies, angelic mediators, as links in the chain which should bind man to God. They still failed to realize the majesty and significance, the completeness, of the person of Christ.

Practical Duties Which Arise. And the practical duty also which follows from the recognition of the theological truth is enforced by both apostles in very similar language. St. Paul entreats the Colossians to seek those things which are above, where Christ is seated at the right hand of God (Colossians 3:1), and in the companion letter, which he also tells them to read, he reminds the churches that God raised them with Christ and seated them with him in heavenly places in Christ Jesus (Ephesians 2:6); in the same way St. John gives this promise to the Laodiceans in the name of his Lord: "To him who overcomes, I will give the right to sit with me on my throne, just as I overcame and sat down with my Father on his throne" (Revelation 3:21).

Warning Against Lukewarmness. Again, after a parting greeting to the church of Laodicea, St. Paul closes with a warning to Archippus, apparently its chief pastor, to see to it that he "complete the work" (Colossians 4:17). Some signs of waning zeal seem to be behind this rebuke. It may be an accidental coincidence, but it is at least worth noting that lukewarmness is the particular sin denounced by the angel of the Laodiceans and that the necessity of greater earnestness is the burden of the message to that church (Revelation 3:19). As with the people, so it is with the priest. The community takes its color from and communicates its color to its spiritual rulers. The "be zealous" of St. John is the counterpart to the "take heed" of St. Paul.

Pride over Wealth Is Denounced. Lastly, in the message from the book of Revelation the pride of wealth is sternly condemned in the Laodicean church (Revelation 3:17-18). The proud vaunt of the Laodiceans receives its best illustration from an event at Laodicea. Only a few years before, an earthquake had laid the city in ruins. Yet from this catastrophe she rose again with more than her former splendor. This, however, was not her chief claim for respect. While other cities, prostrated by a similar visitation, had sought relief from the concessions of the Roman senate or the liberality of the emperor's purse, it was the glory of Laodicea that she alone neither courted nor obtained assistance but recovered by her own resources. Thus she had asserted a proud independence to which neither far-famed metropolitan Ephesus, nor old imperial Sardis, nor her prosperous commercial neighbors Apamea and Cibyra could lay claim. No one would dispute her boast, "I am rich; I have acquired wealth and do not need a thing" (Revelation 3:17).

The Pride of Intellectual Wealth. But is there not a second and subsidiary idea underlying the rebuke found in the book of Revelation? The pride of intellectual wealth, we may well suspect, was a temptation at Laodicea hardly less strong than the pride of material resources. When St. Paul wrote, the theology of the Gospel and the comprehension of the church were alike endangered by a spirit of intellectual exclusiveness in these cities. He warned them against a vain philosophy, against a show of wisdom, against an intrusive mystic speculation which vainly puffed up the selfish mind (Colossians 2:8, 18, 23). He tacitly contrasted with this false intellectual wealth "the glorious riches of this mystery, which is Christ in you" (Colossians 1:27)—the riches of full assurance of understanding, the genuine treasures of wisdom and knowledge (Colossians 2:2-3). May not the same contrast be seen in St. John's language? The Laodiceans boast of their enlightenment, but they are blind, and to cure their blindness they must seek ointment for their eyes from the hands of the Physician. They vaunt their wealth of knowledge, but they were wretched paupers and must beg the refined gold of the Gospel to relieve their needs (compare Ephesians 1:18).

The Obscurity of Colosse

Laodicea and Hierapolis held the foremost place in the records of the early church and continued to bear an active, though inconspicuous, part in later Christian history; but Colosse was from the very first a cipher. The town itself was already waning in importance when the apostle wrote, and its subsequent decline seems to have been very rapid. Not a single event in Christian history is connected with its name; and its every existence is only rescued from oblivion when at long intervals some bishop of Colosse signs a decree of an ecclesiastical synod. The city ceased to strike coins in Gordian's reign (A.D. 238-244). It fell gradually into decay, being supplanted by the neighboring town Chonae, the modern Chonos, so called from the natural funnels through which streams here disappear in underground channels formed by the incrustations of travertine. We may conjecture also that its ruin was hastened by a renewed assault of its ancient enemy, the earthquake.

Turkish Conquest

The Turkish conquest pressed more than common severity on these districts. When the day of visitation came, the church was taken by surprise. Occupied with ignoble quarrels and selfish interests, she had no ear for the voice of him who demanded admission. The door was barred and the knock unheeded. The long-impending doom overtook her, and the golden candlestick was removed forever from the eternal presence.

2

The Colossian
Heresy

From the language St. Paul wrote to the church of Colosse, we may infer the presence of two disturbing elements which threatened the purity of Christian faith and practice in that community. These elements can be differentiated from each other, though it does not follow that they present the teaching of two distinct parties.

Judaic Element

A mere glance at the letter suffices to detect the presence of Judaism in the teaching which the apostle combats. The observance of sabbaths and new moons is decisive in this respect. The distinction of meats and drinks points in the same direction (Colossians 2:16-17, 21ff.). Even the enforcement of the initiatory rite of Judaism may be inferred from the contrast implied in St. Paul's recommendation of spiritual circumcision (Colossians 2:11).

Gnostic Element

On the other hand, a closer examination of the letter's language shows that these Judaic features do not exhaust the scope of the heresy or heresies against which the letter is directed. We discern an element of theosophic speculation which is alien to the spirit of Judaism proper. We are confronted with a shadowy mysticism which loses itself in the contemplation of the unseen world. We discover a tendency to interpose certain spiritual agencies, intermediate beings, between God and man as the instruments of communication and the objects of worship (Colossians 2:4, 8, 18, 23). Anticipating the result which will appear more clearly later, we may say that along with its Judaism there was a Gnostic element in the false teaching which prevailed at Colosse.

Are These Combined or Separate?

Have we then two heresies here or only one? Were these elements distinct, or were they fused into the same system? In other words, is St. Paul opposing a phase of Judaism on the one hand and a phase of Gnosticism on the other, or did he find himself in conflict with a Judeo-Gnostic heresy which combined the two?

General Reasons for Supposing One Heresy Only, in Which They Are Fused

On closer examination we find ourselves compelled to adopt the latter alternative. The letter itself contains no hint that the apostle has more than one set of antagonists in view; and the needless multiplication of people or events is always to be deprecated in historical criticism. Nor indeed does the hypothesis of a single complex heresy present any real difficulty. If the two elements seem irreconcilable, or at least incongruous, at first sight, the incongruity disappears on further examination. It will be shown in the course of this investigation that some special tendencies of religious thought among the Jews themselves before and about this time prepared the way for such a combination in a Christian community like the church of Colosse. Moreover, we shall find that the Christian heresies of the succeeding ages exhibit in a more developed form the same complex type which here appears in its nascent state. This later development not only shows that the combination was historically possible in itself but likewise presupposes some earlier state of its existence such as confronts us at Colosse.

St. Paul's Language Is Decisive on This Point

The apostle's language hardly leaves the question open. The two elements are so closely interwoven in his refutation that it is impossible to separate them. He passes backward and forward from the one to the other in such a way as to show that they are only parts of one complex whole. On this point the logical connection of the sentences is decisive:

> . . . *See to it that no one takes you captive through hollow and deceptive philosophy, which depends on human tradition and the basic principles of*

this world rather than on Christ. For in Christ all the fullness of the Deity lives in bodily form, and you have been given fullness in Christ, who is the head over every power and authority. In him you were also circumcised, in the putting off of the sinful nature, not with a circumcision done by the hands of men but with the circumcision done by Christ, having been buried with him in baptism and raised with him through your faith in the power of God, who raised him from the dead. When you were dead in your sins and in the uncircumcision of your sinful nature, God made you alive with Christ. He forgave us all our sins, having canceled the written code, with its regulations, that was against us and that stood opposed to us; he took it away, nailing it to the cross. . . . Therefore do not let anyone judge you by what you eat or drink, or with regard to a religious festival, a New Moon celebration or a Sabbath day. . . . Do not let anyone who delights in false humility and the worship of angels disqualify you for the prize. . . . Since you died with Christ to the basic principles of this world, why, as though you still belonged to it, do you submit to its rules. . . ? Such regulations indeed have an appearance of wisdom, with their self-imposed worship, their false humility and their harsh treatment of the body, but they lack any value in restraining sensual indulgence.

—Colossians 2:2-23

Here the superior wisdom, the speculative element which is characteristic of Gnosticism, and the ritual observance, the practical element which was supplied by Judaism, are regarded not only as springing from the same stem but also as intertwined in their growth. And the more carefully we examine the sequence of the apostle's thoughts, the closer the link will appear.

Gnosticism Must Be Defined and Described

Having described the speculative element in this complex heresy provisionally as Gnostic, I propose to inquire in the first place how far Judaism prior to and independently of Christianity had allied itself with Gnostic thinking, and then whether the description of the Colossians' heresy is such as to justify us in thus classing it as a species of Gnosticism. But as a preliminary to these inquiries, some definition of the word, or at least some conception of the leading ideas which it involves, will be necessary.

The Intellectual Exclusiveness of Gnosticism

The name *Gnosticism* implies the possession of a superior wisdom which is hidden from others. It makes a distinction between the select few who have this higher gift and the common majority who are without it. Faith, blind faith, suffices the latter, while knowledge is the exclusive possession of the former. Thus it recognizes a separation of an intellectual caste in religion, introducing the distinction of an esoteric and an exoteric doctrine and interposing an initiation of some kind or other between the two classes. In short, it is animated by the exclusive aristocratic spirit which distinguishes the ancient religions and from which it was a main function of Christianity to deliver mankind.

Speculative Tenets of Gnosticism

This was its spirit. The intellectual questions on which its energies were concentrated and to which it professed to hold the key were mainly twofold: how can the work of creation be explained? and how can we account for the existence of evil? To reconcile the creation of the world and the existence of evil with the conception of God as the absolute Being was the problem which all the Gnostic systems set themselves to solve. It will be seen that the two questions cannot be treated independently but have a very close and intimate connection with each other.

How to Explain the Existence of Evil. The Gnostic argument ran as follows: Did God create the world out of nothing, evolve it from himself? Then, God being perfectly good and creation having resulted from his sole act without any opposing or modifying influence, evil would have been impossible; otherwise we are driven to the conclusion that God created evil.

Matter the Abode of Evil. This solution being rejected as impossible, the Gnostic was obliged to postulate some antagonistic principle independent of God by which his creative energy was thwarted and limited. This opposing principle, the kingdom of evil, he conceived to be the world of matter. Precisely how it operated varied in different Gnostic systems. It is sometimes thought of as a dead passive resistance, sometimes as a turbulent active power. But though the exact point of view might vary, the object contemplated is always the same. In some way or other evil is regarded as residing in the material, sensible world. Thus Gnostic speculation on the existence of evil ends in a dualism.

How to Explain Creation. This point being conceded, the ulterior question arises: How then is creation possible? How can the Infinite communicate with the finite, the good with the evil? How can God act upon matter? God is perfect, absolute, incomprehensible.

Doctrine of Emanations. This, the Gnostic went on to argue, could only have been possible by some self-limitation on the part of God. God must express himself in some way. There must be some evolution, some effluence, of deity. Thus the divine being germinates, as it were; and the first germination again evolves a second from itself in like manner. In this way we obtain a series of successive emanations which may be more or fewer as the requirements of any particular system demand. In each successive evolution the divine element is feebler. They sink gradually lower and lower in the scale as they are farther removed from their source, until at last contact with matter is possible, and creation ensues. These are the emanations, aeons, spirits, or angels of Gnosticism, conceived as more or less concrete and personal according to the different aspects in which they are regarded in different systems.

Practical Errors of Gnosticism

Such is the bare outline of the speculative views of Gnosticism. But it is obvious that these views must have exerted a powerful influence on the ethical systems of their advocates, and thus they would involve important practical consequences. If matter is the principle of evil, it is of infinite moment for a person to know how he can avoid its baneful influence and thus keep his higher nature unclogged and unsullied.

Two Opposite Ethical Rules. Rigid asceticism. On the one hand, it was thought that the desired end might be best achieved by a rigorous abstinence. Thus communication with matter, if it could not be entirely avoided, might be reduced to a minimum. Its worst defilements might at least be avoided. The material part of a person would be subdued and mortified, if it could not be annihilated; and the spirit, thus set free, would be sublimated and rise to its correct level. Thus the ethics of Gnosticism pointed in the first instance to a strict asceticism.

Unrestrained license. But obviously the results thus attained are very slight and inadequate. Matter is around us everywhere. We do but touch the skirts of the evil when we endeavor to fence ourselves about by prohibitive ordinances, as, for instance, when we enforce a strict diet or forbid marriage. Some more comprehensive rule is needed which will apply to every contingency and every moment of our lives. Arguing in this way, other Gnostic teachers arrived at an ethical rule directly opposed to the former. "Cultivate an entire indifference," they said, "to the world of sense. Do not give it a thought one way or the other, but follow your own impulses. The ascetic principle assigns a certain importance to matter. So the ascetic fails to assert his own independence. The true rule of life is to treat matter as something alien to you, toward which you have no duties or obligations and which you can use or leave unused as you like." In this way the reaction from rigid asceticism led to the opposite extreme of unrestrained licentiousness, both springing from the same false conception of matter as the principle of evil.

The Original Independence of Gnosticism and Its Subsequent Link with Christianity

Gnosticism, as defined by these characteristic features, obviously has no necessary link with Christianity. Christianity would naturally arouse it to unwonted activity by leading people to dwell more earnestly on the nature and power of evil and thus stimulating more systematic thought on the theological questions which had already taken their attention. After a short time Gnosticism would absorb into its system a number of Christian elements, or Christianity in some of its forms would be influenced by Gnosticism. But the thing itself had an independent root and seems to have been first in time. The probabilities of the case, and the scanty traditions of history, alike point to this independence of the two. If so, it is a matter of little moment at what precise time the name *Gnostic* was adopted, whether before or after contact with Christianity, for we are concerned only with the growth and direction of thought which the name represents.

Its Alliance with Judaism Before Christianity

If then Gnosticism was not an offspring of Christianity but a direction of religious speculation which existed independently, we are at liberty to entertain the question whether it did not form an alliance with Christianity. There is at least no obstacle which bars such an investigation at the outset. If this should prove to be the case, then we have a combination which prepares the way for the otherwise strange phenomena presented in the letter to the Colossians.

The Three Sects of the Jews

Those who have sought analogies to the three Jewish sects among the philosophical schools of Greece and Rome have compared the Sadducees to the Epicureans, the Pharisees to the Stoics, and the Essenes to the Pythagoreans. Like all historical parallels, this comparison is open to misunderstanding. But carefully used, the illustration is pertinent and instructive.

Sadduceeism, Purely Negative. With the Sadducees we have no concern here. Whatever respect may be due to their attitude in the earlier stages of their history, by the Christian era at least they had ceased to deserve our sympathy. Their position had become mostly negative. They took their stand on denials—the denial of the existence of angels, the denial of the resurrection of the dead, the denial of progressive development in the Jewish church. In these negative tendencies, in the materialistic teaching of the sect, and in the moral consequences to which it led, a very rough likeness to the Epicureans did transpire.

Pharisaism and Essenism Compared. The two positive sects were the Pharisees and the Essenes. Both were strict observers of the ritual law; but while the Pharisee was essential practical, the tendency of the Essene was toward mysticism; while the Pharisee was a man of the world, the Essene was a member of a brotherhood. In this respect the Stoic and the Pythagorean were the nearest counterparts which the history of Greek philosophy and social life could offer.

Elusive Features of Essenism. While the portrait of the Pharisee is distinctly traced and easily recognized, this is not the case with the Essene. The Essene is the great enigma of Hebrew history. Admired alike by Jew, by heathen, and by Christian, he yet remains a dim vague outline on which the highest subtlety of successive critics has been employed to supply a substantial form and an adequate coloring. An ascetic, mystical, dreamy recluse, he seems too far removed from the hard experience of life to be capable of realization.

And yet by careful use of the existing materials a portrait of this sect may be restored to establish with a reasonable amount of probability the point with which we are alone here concerned. From the delineations of ancient writers, especially Philo and Josephus, it is seen that the characteristic feature of Essenism was a particular direction of mystic speculation involving a rigid asceticism as its practical consequence. Following the definition of Gnosticism which has been already given, we may not unfitly call this tendency Gnostic.

Main Features of Essenism

Having in this statement anticipated the results, I will now endeavor to develop the main features of Essenism; and in doing so, we will bear in mind the portrait of the Colossian heresy in St. Paul and note the resemblances, as the inquiry proceeds.

The Judaic element is especially prominent in the life and teaching of the sect. The Essene was exceptionally rigorous in his observance of the Mosaic ritual. In his strict abstinence from work on the Sabbath he far surpassed all the other Jews. He would not light a fire, would not move a vessel, would not perform even the most ordinary functions of life. The whole day was given up to religious exercises and to exposition of the Scriptures. His respect for the law extended also to the lawgiver. After God, the name of Moses was held in the highest reverence. He who blasphemed his name was punished with death. In all these points the Essene was an exaggeration, almost a caricature, of the Pharisee.

So far the Essene has not departed from the principles of normal Judaism; but here the divergence begins. In three main points we trace the working of influences which must have been derived from external sources.

Rigid Asceticism Over Marriage, Food, and Oil for Anointing. To the legalism of the Pharisee, the Essene added an asceticism which was peculiarly his own and which in many respects contradicted the tenets of the other sect. The honorable, and even exaggerated, estimate of marriage which was characteristic of the Jew, and of the Pharisee as the typical Jew, found no favor with the Essene. Marriage was to him an abomination. Those Essenes who lived together as members of an order and in whom the principles of the sect were carried to their logical conclusion eschewed it altogether. Woman was a mere instrument of temptation in their eyes—deceitful, faithless, selfish, jealous, misled, and misleading by her passions.

But their ascetic tendencies did not stop here. The Pharisee was very careful to observe the distinction between lawful and unlawful meats, as laid down by the Mosaic code, and even added to these ordinances minute regulations of his own. But the Essene went far beyond him. He drank no wine; he did not touch animal food. His meal consisted of a piece of bread and a single dish of vegetables.

In hot climates, oil for anointing the body is almost a necessity of life. From this too the Essenes totally abstained. Even if they were accidentally smeared, they were careful at once to wash themselves, holding the mere touch to be a contamination.

From these facts it seems clear that Essene abstinence was something more than the mere exaggeration of Pharisaic principles. The rigor of the Pharisee was based on his obligation of obedience to an absolute external law. The Essene introduced a new principle. He condemned in any form the gratification of the natural cravings. They were evil in themselves. In short, in the asceticism of the Essene we seem to see the germ of that Gnostic dualism which regards matter as the principle, or at least the abode, of evil.

Speculative Tenets. As we investigate the speculative tenets of the sect, we see that the Essenes have diverged greatly from the common type of Jewish orthodoxy.

Tendency toward sun-worship. At dawn they addressed certain prayers to the Sun, "as if entreating him to rise." They were careful to conceal and bury all polluting substances, so they did "not insult the rays of the god." They may not have thought of the sun as more than a symbol of the unseen power who gives light and life; but their outward demonstrations of reverence were sufficiently prominent to give them the epithet of "Sun-worshipers."

Resurrection of the body denied. It is significant that while the Pharisee believed in the resurrection of the body as a cardinal article of faith, the Essene restricted himself to a belief in the immortality of the soul. The soul, he maintained, was confined in the body as in a prison. Only when the soul was disentangled from these fetters of the body would it be truly free. Then it would soar aloft, rejoicing in its newly attained liberty. This teaching ties in with their fundamental conception in the malignity of matter. To those who believed in this, the resurrection of the body would be repulsive, as it involved a perpetuation of evil.

Prohibition of sacrifices. The Essenes separated themselves more noticeably from the religious belief of the orthodox Jew in another way. While they sent gifts to the Temple at Jerusalem, they refused to offer sacrifices there. It would appear that the slaughter of animals was altogether forbidden by their creed.

Esoteric teaching about angels. When a novice was to be admitted into the full privileges of the order, the oath of admission bound him ". . . to guard carefully the books of their sect, and the names of the angels." More is hidden in this last expression than meets the eye. This esoteric doctrine relating to angelic beings may have been another link between Essenism and the religion of Zoroaster. At all events there seems to be linked the self-imposed service and worshiping of angels at Colosse; and we may well suspect that we have here a germ which was developed into the Gnostic doctrine of emanations.

Magic charms. The Essenes studied with extraordinary diligence the writings of the ancients, from where they learned about the properties of roots and stones. This points to the study of occult sciences and is similar to the practice of magical arts, which was a characteristic of Gnosticism and is condemned by Christian teachers even in the heresies of the apostolic age.

The Exclusive Spirit of Essenism. The Essenes had an esoteric teaching which they regarded as the exclusive possession of the privileged few. Their "mysteries" were not allowed to be told to the uninitiated. Their whole organization was arranged to prevent the divulgence of its secrets to those outside its ranks.

Thus, the three characteristics which were singled out above as distinctive of Gnosticism reappear in the Essenes. This Jewish sect exhibits the same exclusiveness in the communication of its doctrines. Its theological speculations take the same direction, dwelling on the mysteries of creation, regarding matter as the abode of evil, and postulating certain intermediate spiritual agencies as necessary links of communication between heaven and earth. And, lastly, its speculative opinions involve the same ethical conclusions and lead in like manner to a rigid asceticism.

The Dispersion of the Essenes

When I speak of the Judaism in the Colossian church as Essene, I do not assume a precise identity of origin but only an essential affinity of type with the Essenes of the mother country. As a matter of history, it may or may not have sprung from the colonies on the shores of the Dead Sea. All along its frontier, wherever Judaism became enamored with and was wedded to oriental mysticism, the same union would produce substantially the same results.

When St. Paul visits Ephesus, he comes into contact with certain strolling Jews, exorcists, who attempt to cast out evil spirits (Acts 19:13). According to Josephus, these kinds of exorcisms were especially practiced by the Essenes. It is also worth observing that the next incident in St. Luke's narrative is the burning of magical books by those whom St. Paul converted on this occasion (Acts 19:18-19). As Jews are especially mentioned among these converts, and as the books of charms are ascribed to the Essenes by Josephus, the two incidents, coming next to each other, throw great light on the type of Judaism which thus appears at Ephesus.

Three Characteristics of Colossian Gnosticism

So far it has been shown, first, that Essene Judaism was Gnostic in its character, and, second, that this type of Jewish thought and practice had established itself in the apostolic age in those parts of Asia Minor with which we are more directly concerned. Now we turn to examine the nature of the Colossian heresy more closely and whether it deserves to be given the name of Gnostic Judaism. Its Judaism all will agree with. Its claim to be regarded as Gnostic will require a closer scrutiny. And in this investigation we follow the three characteristics of Gnosticism again and see how far they are relevant.

Intellectual Exclusiveness

Gnosticism tried to establish, or rather preserve, an intellectual oligarchy in religion. It had its hidden wisdom, its exclusive mysteries, its privileged class. In St. Paul's letter to the Colossians he feels himself challenged to contend for the universality of the Gospel. This indeed is a characteristic feature of the apostle's teaching at all times, but note here that the apostle changes his method of defending it. This fact suggests that there has been a change in the direction of the attack. It is no longer against national exclusiveness but against intellectual exclusiveness that he fights. His adversaries now erect an artificial barrier of spiritual privilege. It is not now against the Jew as such, but against the Jew become Gnostic that he fights the battle of liberty.

In other words, it is not against Christian Pharisaism but against Christian Essenism that he defends his position. Only in the light of such an antagonism can we understand his emphatic iteration with which he claims to warn "everyone with all wisdom" and "present everyone perfect in Christ"

(Colossians 1:28). Remember that "wisdom" in Gnostic teaching was the exclusive possession of the few and that "perfection" was the term especially applied in their language to this privileged minority. This shows why St. Paul should go on to say that this universality of the Gospel is the one object of his contention, to which all the energies of his life are directed, and having done so, should express his intense concern for the churches of Colosse and the neighborhood, in case they should be led astray by a spurious wisdom to desert the true knowledge (Colossians 1:29; 2:1-4).

This danger will also help us to appreciate another novel feature of this letter. While concentrating on the removal of all distinctions in Christ, he repeats his earlier contrasts: "Greek or Jew," "circumcised or uncircumcised," "slave or free"; but to these he adds new words which immediately give a wider scope and more immediate application of the lesson. In Christ the existence of "barbarian" and even "Scythian," the lowest type of barbarian, is obliterated (Colossians 3:11). As culture, civilization, philosophy, and knowledge are no conditions of acceptance, so neither is their absence any disqualification in the believer. The aristocracy of intellectual discernment which Gnosticism upheld in religion is abhorrent to the first principles of the Gospel.

True and False Wisdom Contrasted. We must also explain the frequent occurrence of the words "wisdom" (Colossians 1:9, 28; 2:3; 3:16;), "understanding" (Colossians 1:9; 2:2), "knowledge" (Colossians 1:9-10; 2:3) in this letter. St. Paul takes up the language of his opponents and translates it into a higher realm. The false teachers propose a "philosophy," but it was only an empty deceit, only a plausible display of false reasoning (see Colossians 2:4, 8). They pretended "wisdom," but it was merely a profession, not a reality (Colossians 2:23). Against these pretensions the apostle sets the true wisdom of the Gospel. On its wealth, its fullness, its perfection, he is never tired of dwelling (Colossians 1:9, 28; 3:16). The true wisdom, he would argue, is essentially spiritual and yet essentially definite, while the false argument is speculative, vague, and dreamy (Colossians 2:4, 18).

They also had their rites of initiation. St. Paul contrasts these with the one universal, all-embracing mystery (Colossians 1:26-27; 2:2; 4:3), the knowledge of God in Christ. This mystery is complete in itself. It contains "all the treasures of wisdom and knowledge" (Colossians 2:3). Moreover, it is offered to all without distinction. Though once hidden, its revelation is unrestricted, except by the waywardness and disobedience of people. The esoteric spirit of Gnosticism finds no countenance in the apostle's teaching.

Speculative Tenets

From the informing spirit of Gnosticism we turn to the speculative tenets—the cosmogony and theology of the Gnostic.

Here, too, the affinities to Gnosticism reveal themselves in the Colossian heresy. We cannot fail to observe that the apostle has in view the doctrine of intermediate agencies, regarded as instruments in the creation and government of the world. Though this tenet is not directly mentioned, it is tacitly assumed in St. Paul's teaching as he opposes it. Against the philosophy of successive evolutions from the divine nature, angelic mediators forming the successive links in the chain which binds the finite to the Infinite, St. Paul sets the doctrine of the one eternal Son, the Word of God begotten before the creation of the world (see the two great christological passages in Colossians—1:15-20; 2:9-15).

The angelology of the heretics had a twofold bearing: it was closely connected with both cosmogony and with religion. St. Paul also shows the mediatorial work of Christ as twofold: it is exercised in the natural creation, and it is exercised in the spiritual creation. In both these spheres Christ's initiative is absolute, his control is universal, and his action is complete. By his agency the world of matter was created and sustained. He is both the beginning and the end of the material universe (see Colossians 1:16). Nor is his office in the spiritual world less complete. In the church, as in the universe, he is sole, absolute, supreme—the primary source from which all life proceeds and the ultimate arbiter in whom all feuds are reconciled.

Christ's Relationship to Deity: As God Manifested. On the one hand, in his relationship to the Deity Christ is the visible image of the invisible God. He is not only the chief manifestation of the divine nature—in him resides the totality of the divine powers and attributes. For this totality Gnostic teachers had a technical term, the *pleroma* or *plenitude*. From the *pleroma* they supposed that all those agencies issued through which God has at any time exerted his power in creation or manifested his will through revelation. This *pleroma* was distributed, diluted, transformed, and darkened by foreign admixture. They were only partial and blurred images, often deceptive caricatures, of their original, broken lights of the great central Light. It is not improbable that, like later speculators of the same school, they found a place somewhere or other in their genealogy of spiritual beings for Christ. If so, St. Paul's language becomes doubly significant. In contrast to their teaching, St. Paul asserts, and repeats the assertion, that the *pleroma* abides absolutely and wholly in Christ as the Word of God (1:19). The entire light is concentrated in him.

Christ's Relationship to Created Things: As Absolute Lord. Hence it follows that, as regards created things, Christ's supremacy must be absolute. In heaven as in earth, over things immaterial as over things material, he is King. Speculations on the nature of intermediate spiritual agencies—their names, their ranks, their offices—were rife in the schools of Judeo-Gnostic thought. "Thrones, dominations, princedoms, virtues, powers"—these formed part of the spiritual nomenclature which they had invented to describe grades of angelic mediators. Without entering into these speculations, the apostle asserts that Christ is Lord of all, the highest and lowest, whatever rank they may hold and by whatever name they are called (1:16), for they are parts of creation, and he is the source of creation. Through him they became, and unto him they tend.

Angelolatry Is Condemned. Hence the worship of angels, which the false teachers inculcated, was utterly wrong in principle. The motive of this angelolatry is not difficult to imagine. There was a show of humility (2:18), for there was a confession of weakness in this subservience to inferior mediatorial agencies. It was possible to grasp at the lower links of the chain which bound earth to heaven, when heaven itself seemed far beyond the reach of man. The successive grades of intermediate beings were successive steps by which man might mount the ladder leading up to God's throne. This carefully woven web of sophistry the apostle tears to shreds. The doctrine of the false teachers was based on confident assumptions about angelic beings of whom they could know nothing. It was moreover a denial of Christ's twofold personality and his mediatorial office. It follows from the true conception of Christ's person that he and he alone can bridge the chasm between earth and heaven, for he is at once the lowest and the highest. He raises man up to God, and he brings God down to man. Thus the chain is reduced to a single link, this link being the Word made flesh. As the *pleroma* resides in him, so is it communicated to us through him (2:10; compare 1:9). To substitute allegiance to any other spiritual mediator is to sever the link of the limbs with the Head, who is the center of life and the mainspring of all energy throughout the body (2:19).

The Apostle's Practical Inference. Hence follows the practical conclusion that whatever is done must be done in the name of the Lord (3:17). Wives must submit to their husbands "in the Lord"; children must obey their parents "in the Lord"; servants must work for their masters as working "for the Lord" (3:18, 20, 23). The mentioning of "in the Lord," "for the Lord" is not an irrelevant form of words but arises as an immediate inference from the main idea which underlies the doctrinal part of the letter.

Moral Results of Gnostic Teaching

Speculative tenets of Gnosticism might lead, and did lead, to either of two practical extremes—to rigid asceticism or to unbridled license. The latter alternative appears to some extent in the heresy of the Pastoral Letters (see

2 Timothy 3:1-7) and still more clearly in the general epistles (see 2 Peter 2:10ff.; Jude 8) and the book of Revelation (Revelation 2:14, 20-22).

Asceticism of the Colossian Heresy Not Explained by Its Judaism. But the former and nobler extreme was the first impulse of the Gnostic. To escape from the infection of evil by escaping from the domination of matter was his chief worry. This appears very clearly in the Colossian heresy. Though the prohibitions to which the apostle alludes might be explained in part by the ordinances of the Mosaic ritual, this explanation will not cover all the facts. Thus, for instance, drinks are mentioned as well as meats (2:16), though on the former the law of Moses is silent. Thus again the rigorous denunciation, "'Do not handle! Do not taste! Do not touch!'" (2:21) seems to go way beyond the levitical enactments. Moreover, the motive of these prohibitions is Essene rather than Pharisaic, Gnostic rather than Jewish. These severities of discipline were intended to restrain "sensual indulgence" (2:23). They professed to treat the body with entire disregard, to ignore its cravings, and to deny its needs. In short, they betray a strong ascetic tendency, of which normal Judaism, as represented by the Pharisee, offers no explanation.

The Gnosticism of the Colossians Is Vague and Undeveloped. The elements of Gnostic theory crystallized around the facts of the Gospel. So we still seem justified in speaking of these general ideas as Gnostic, guarding ourselves at the same time against misunderstanding with the double caution that we use the term to express the simplest and most elementary conceptions of this tendency of thought and that we do not postulate its use as a distinct name for any sect or sects at this early date. Thus limited, the view that the writer of this letter is combating a Gnostic heresy seems free from all objections, while it at the same time explains his choice of words. And certainly it does not place any weapon in the hands of those who would assail the early date and apostolic authorship of the letter.

3

Character and Contents
of the Letter

Without the preceding investigation the teaching of this letter would be very imperfectly understood, for its direction was necessarily determined by the occasion which gave rise to it. Only when we have once grasped the nature of the teaching which St. Paul is combating do we perceive that every sentence is vibrant with life and meaning.

The Errors Though Twofold Sprang from One Root

The error of the heretical teachers was twofold. They had a false conception in theology, and they had a false basis of morals. These two were closely linked together and had their root in the same fundamental error, the idea of matter as the abode of evil and thus antagonistic to God.

The Answer to Both Is the Same Truth

As the two elements of the heretical teaching were derived from the same source, so the reply to both was sought by the apostle in the same idea—the conception of the person of Christ as the one absolute mediator between God and man, the true and only reconciler of heaven and earth.

But though they are thus ultimately linked, it is still necessary for a better appreciation of St. Paul's position to deal with them separately and to consider first the theological and then the ethical teaching of the letter.

The Theological Error of the Heretics

This Colossian heresy was no coarse and vulgar development of falsehood.

It soared far above the Pharisaic Judaism which St. Paul refutes in the letter to the Galatians. The question in which it was interested lies at the very root of our religious consciousness. The impulse was given to its speculations by an overwhelming sense of the unapproachable majesty of God but an instinctive recognition of the chasm which separates God from man, God from the world, and God from matter. Its energy was sustained by the intense yearning after some mediation which might span the gap and establish communion between the finite and the Infinite. Up to this point it was deeply religious in the best sense of the term.

The answer which it gave to these questions failed signally in two respects. On the one hand, it was drawn from the atmosphere of mystical speculation. It had no foundation in history and made no appeal to experience. On the other hand, notwithstanding its complexity, it was unsatisfactory in its results, for in this plurality of mediators none was competent to meet the requirements of the case. God here and man there—no angel or spirit, whether one or more, being neither God nor man, could truly reconcile the two.

St. Paul's Answer Is in the Person of Christ. The apostle pointed out to the Colossians a more excellent way. It was the great purpose of Christianity to satisfy those very yearnings which were working in their hearts, to solve that very problem which had exercised their minds. In Christ they would find the answer they sought. His life—his cross and resurrection—was the guarantee; his Person—the Word incarnate—was the solution. He alone filled up, he alone could fill up, the void which lay between God and man, spanning the gulf which separated the Creator and creation. This solution offered by the Gospel is as simple as it is adequate. To their cosmical speculations and to their religious yearnings alike, Jesus Christ is the true answer. In the world, as in the church, Christ is the one and only mediator, the one and only reconciler. This twofold idea runs like a double thread through the fabric of the apostle's teaching in those passages of the letter where he is describing the Person of Christ.

It is convenient, in order to better understand St. Paul's teaching, to consider these two aspects of Christ's mediation separately—its function in the natural and in the spiritual order respectively.

In the universe. The heresy of the Colossian teachers came from their cosmical speculations. Therefore, it was natural for the apostle, in his reply, to stress the function of the Word in the creation and rule of the world. This is the aspect of Christ's work most prominent in the first of the two distinctly christological passages (1:15-20). Everything was created by him, is sustained by him, and leads to him. Thus Christ is the beginning, the middle, and the end of creation. He is this because he is the very image of the invisible God, because in him dwells the plenitude of Deity.

In the church. But if Christ's mediatorial office in the physical creation was the starting point of the apostle's teaching, his mediatorial office in the spiritual creation is its principal theme. The cosmogonies of the false teachers were framed not so much in the interests of philosophy as in the interests of religion; and the apostle replies to them in the same spirit and with the same motive. If the function of Christ is unique in the universe, so is it also in the church. He is the sole and absolute link between God and humanity. Nothing short of his personality would suffice as the medium of reconciliation between the two. Nothing short of his life and work in the flesh, as consummated in his person, would serve as an assurance of God's love and pardon. His cross is the atonement of mankind with God. He is the Head with whom all the living members of the body are in direct and immediate communication, who suggests their many activities to each other, who directs their different functions in subordination to the healthy working of the whole, from whom they individually receive their inspiration and their strength.

So Angelic Mediations Are Fundamentally Wrong. Since Christ is all this, he cannot consent to share his prerogative with others. He absorbs in himself the whole function of mediation. Through him alone, without any interposing link, the human soul has access to the Father. Here was the true answer to those deep yearnings after spiritual communion with God which sought and could not find satisfaction in the many and fantastic creations of a dreamy mysticism. The worship of angels might give the appearance of humility; but it was in reality a contemptible defiance of the fundamental idea of the Gospel, a flat denial of the absolute character of Christ's person and office. It was a severance of the correct link with the Head, an amputation of the disordered limb, which was thus cut off from the source of life and left to perish for lack of spiritual nourishment.

The Ethical Error of the Heretics

When we turn from the theology of these Colossian heretics to their ethical teaching, we find it characterized by the same earnestness. Of them it might indeed be said that they did "hunger and thirst after righteousness." Escape from impurity, immunity from evil, was a passion with them. But it was no less true that notwithstanding all their sincerity, they went astray in the wilderness; hungry and thirsty, their soul fainted within them. By their fatal transference of the abode of sin from the human heart within to the material world without, they had incapacitated themselves from finding the true antidote. Where they placed the evil, there they necessarily sought the remedy. Hence they attempted to fence themselves around and to purify their lives by a code of rigorous prohibitions. Their energy was expended on battling with the physical conditions of human life. Their whole mind was absorbed in the struggle with imaginary forms of evil.

So their characters were molded by the thoughts which habitually engaged them. Since the "basic principles of this world," the things that are "all destined to perish with use" (2:20, 22), engrossed all their attention, it could not fail but that they should be dragged down from the serene heights of the spiritual life into the cloudy atmosphere which shrouds this lower earth.

St. Paul Substitutes a Principle for Ordinances

St. Paul sets himself to combat this false tendency. For negative prohibitions he substitutes a positive principle; for special enactments, a comprehensive motive. He tells them that all their scrupulous restrictions are vain because they fail to touch the springs of action. If they would overcome the evil, they must strike at the root of the evil. Their point of view must be entirely changed. They must transfer themselves into a wholly new sphere of energy. This transference is nothing less than a journey from earth to heaven—from the region of the external and transitory to the region of the spiritual and eternal (3:1ff.). For a code of rules they must substitute a principle of life which is one in its essence but infinite in its application, which will meet every emergency, will control every action, will resist every form of evil.

This Principle Is the Heavenly Life in Christ

This principle they have in Christ. With him they have died to the world; with him they have risen to God. Christ, the revelation of God's holiness, of God's righteousness, of God's love, is light, is life, is heaven. With him they have been translated into a higher sphere, have been brought face to face with the eternal Presence. Let them only realize this translation. It involves new insight, new motives, new energies. They will no more waste themselves on vexatious special restrictions, for they will be furnished with a higher inspiration which will cover all the minute details of action. They will not exhaust their energies in crushing this or that rising desire, but they will kill the whole body (2:11; 3:5, 9) of their earthly passions through the strong arm of this personal communion with God in Christ.

St. Paul's Teaching About Faith and Deeds Considered in the Light of This Principle

When we once grasp this idea which lies at the root of St. Paul's ethical teaching, the moral difficulty which is supposed to attach to his doctrine of faith and deeds has vanished. It is simply an impossibility that faith should exist without deeds. Though in form he states his doctrine as a relation of contrast between the two, in substance it resolves itself into a question of precedence. Faith and deeds are related as principle and practice. Faith—the repose in the unseen, the recognition of eternal principles of truth and right, the sense of personal obligations to an eternal Being who vindicates these principles—must come first. Faith is not an intellectual assent, nor merely a sympathetic sentiment. It is the absolute surrender of self to the will of a Being who has a right to command this surrender. It is this which puts people into a personal relationship with God, which (in St. Paul's language) justifies them before God. For it touches the springs of their actions; it fastens not on this or that detail of conduct but extends throughout the whole sphere of moral activity; and thus it determines their character as responsible beings in the sight of God.

The Style of This Letter

While the hand of St. Paul is unmistakable throughout this letter, we miss the flow and the versatility of the apostle's earlier letters. A comparison with the letters to the Corinthians and to the Philippians will show the difference. It is distinguished from them by a certain ruggedness of expression. The divergence of style is not greater than will appear in the letters of any active-minded person, written at different times and under different circumstances. The letters which I have selected for contrast suggest that the absence of all personal link with the Colossian church will partially, if not wholly, explain the diminished fluency of this letter. At the same time none of St. Paul's letters are more vigorous in conception or more full of meaning. It is the very compression of the thoughts which creates the difficulty. If there is a lack of fluency, there is not lack of force. Feebleness is the last charge which can be brought against this letter.

Analysis

The following is an analysis of the letter:

Section 1: Introductory (1:1-13)

1:1-2 *Opening salutation.*

1:3-8 *Thanksgiving for the progress of the Colossians so far.*

1:9-12 *Prayer for their future advance in knowledge and well-doing through Christ. (This leads the apostle to speak of Christ as the only path of progress.)*

Section 2: Doctrinal:
The Person and Office of Christ (1:13—2:3)

1:13-14	*Through the Son we have our deliverance, our redemption.*
1:15-19	*The preeminence of the Son.*
1:15-17	*As the Head of the natural creation, the universe.*
1:18	*As the Head of the new moral creation, the church.*
1:19	*Thus he is the first in all things, because the* pleroma *has its abode in him.*
1:20—2:3	*The work of the Son—a work of reconciliation.*

	1:20	*Described generally.*
	1:21-23	*Applied specially to the Colossians.*
	1:24-27	*St. Paul's own part in carrying out this work. His sufferings and preaching. The "mystery" with which he is charged.*
	1:28-29	*His anxiety on behalf of all.*
	2:1-3	*And more especially of the Colossian and neighboring churches. (This expression of concern leads him straight on to the next division of the letter.)*

Section 3: Polemical: Warning against errors (2:4—3:4)

2:4-8	*The Colossians charged to abide in the truth of the Gospel as they received it at first, and not to be led astray by a strange philosophy which the new teachers offer.*
2:9-15	*The truth stated first positively and then negatively.*

(In the passage which follows, 2:9-23, it will be observed how St. Paul alternates between the theological and practical bearings of the truth.)

Positively.

	2:9-10	*The* pleroma *dwells wholly in Christ and is communicated through him.*
	2:11-13	*The true circumcision is a spiritual circumcision.*

Negatively. Christ has

	2:14	annulled the law of ordinances.
	2:15	triumphed over all spiritual agencies, however powerful.

2:16—3:4   *Obligations which follow.*

Consequently the Colossians must not

2:16-17   *either submit to ritual prohibitions,*

2:18-19   *or substitute the worship of inferior beings for allegiance to the Head.*

On the contrary this must henceforth be their rule:

2:20-23   *They have died with Christ; and with him they have died to their old life, to earthly ordinances.*

3:1-4   *They have risen with Christ; and with him they have risen to a new life, to heavenly principles.*

Section 4: Hortatory: Practical application of this death and this resurrection (3:5—4:6)

3:5-17   *Comprehensive rules.*

3:5-11   *What vices are to be put off, being mortified in this death.*

3:12-17   *What graces are to be put on, being quickened through his resurrection.*

3:18—4:6   *Special precepts.*

The obligations

3:18-19   *Of wives and husbands.*

3:20-21   *Of children and parents.*

3:22—4:1   *Of slaves and masters.*

4:2-4   *The duty of prayer and thanksgiving; with special intercession on the apostle's behalf.*

4:5-6   *The duty of propriety in behavior towards the unconverted.*

Section 5: Personal (4:7-18)

4:.7-9   *Explanations relating to the letter itself.*

4:10-14   *Greetings from various people.*

4:15-17   *Greetings to various people. A message about Laodicea.*

4:18   *Farewell.*

COLOSSIANS

———

Commentary

Colossians 1:1-14

Opening Greeting (1:1-2)

1-2. Paul, an apostle of Christ Jesus by the will of God, and Timothy our brother, To the holy and faithful brothers in Christ at Colosse: Grace and peace to you from God our Father.

Paul, an apostle of Christ Jesus by no personal merit but by God's gracious will alone, and Timothy, our brother in the faith, to the consecrated people of God in Colosse, the brethren who are steadfast in their allegiance and faithful in Christ. May grace—the well-spring of all mercies—and peace—the crown of all blessings—be bestowed upon you from God our Father.

1. Apostle. On the exceptional omission of this title in some of St. Paul's letters, see Philippians 1:1. Though there is no reason for supposing that his authority was directly impugned in the Colossian church, yet he interposes by virtue of his apostolic commission and therefore uses his authoritative title.

By the will of God. As in 1 Corinthians 1:1, 2 Corinthians 1:1, Ephesians 1:1, 2 Timothy 1:1. These passages show that the words cannot have a polemical bearing. If they had been directed against those who questioned his apostleship, they would probably have taken a stronger form. The expression must therefore be regarded as a renunciation of all personal worth and a declaration of God's unmerited grace; compare Romans 9:16, "It does not, therefore, depend on man's desire or effort, but on God's mercy." The same words **by God's will** are used in other connections in Romans 15:32 and 2 Corinthians 8:5, where no polemical reference is possible.

Timothy. The name of this disciple is attached to the apostle's own in the heading of the Philippian letter, which was probably written at an earlier stage in the apostle's Roman captivity. It appears also in the same connection in the letter to Philemon, but not in the letter to the Ephesians, though these two letters were contemporaneous with one another and with the Colossian letter. For an explanation of the omission, see the introduction on that letter.

In the letters to the Philippians and to Philemon, the presence of Timothy is forgotten at once (see Philippians 1:1). In this letter the plural is maintained throughout the thanksgiving (verses 3, 4, 7, 8, 9) but later dropped when the apostle begins to speak in his own person (1:23-24), and so he continues to the end. The exceptions (1:28; 4:3) *are rather apparent than real.*

Brother. As some designation for Timothy seemed to be required, and as Timothy could not be called an apostle, this, as the simplest title, would naturally suggest itself.

2. The holy. "Saints"—that is, the people consecrated to God, the Israel of the new covenant; see the note on Philippians 1:1. This mode of address marks the later letters of St. Paul. In his earlier letters (1 and 2 Thessalonians, 1 and 2 Corinthians, and Galatians) he writes "the church." The change begins with the letter to the Romans, and from then on the apostle always uses "holy" in various combinations in addressing churches (Romans, Philippians, Colossians, and Ephesians). For a similar phenomenon, serving as a chronological mark, see the note on "greeting" on 4:18.

And faithful brothers. This unusual addition is full of meaning. Some members of the Colossian church were shaken in their allegiance, even if they had not fallen from it. The apostle makes it plain that when he speaks about the holy brothers, saints, he means the true and steadfast members of the brotherhood. In this way he obliquely hints at the defection. So the words **and faithful brothers** are a supplementary explanation of **holy**. He does not directly exclude any, but he indirectly warns all. The epithet **faithful** cannot mean simply "believing," for then it would add nothing which is not already contained in **holy** and **brothers**. Its passive sense, "trustworthy, steadfast, unswerving," must be prominent here, as in Acts 16:15: "If you consider me a believer in the Lord."

In Christ. Most naturally connected with both words in **faithful brothers**, though referring chiefly to **faithful**; compare Ephesians 6:21: "faithful servant in the Lord"; 1 Timothy 1:2: "true son in the faith." For the expression "faithful in Christ Jesus" or, "faithful in the Lord," see also 1 Corinthians 4:17 and Ephesians 1:1. The apostle assumes that the Colossian brethren are steadfast in Christ. Their state thus contrasts with the description of the heretical teacher who (2:19) "has lost connection with the Head."

Our Father. This is the only instance in St. Paul's letters where the name of the Father stands alone in the opening benediction without the addition of Jesus Christ.

Thanksgiving for the Progress of the Colossians So Far (1:3-8)

We always thank God, the Father of our Lord Jesus Christ, when we pray for you, because we have heard of your faith in Christ Jesus and of the love you have for all the saints—the faith and love that spring from the hope that is stored up for you in heaven and that you have already heard about in the word of truth, the gospel that has come to you. All over the world this gospel is bearing fruit and growing, just as it has been doing among you since the day you heard it and understood God's grace in all its truth. You learned it from Epaphras, our dear fellow servant, who is a faithful minister of Christ on our behalf, and who also told us of your love in the Spirit.

We never cease to pour forth our thanksgiving to God, the Father of our Lord Jesus Christ, on your account whenever we pray to him. We are full of thankfulness for the tidings of the faith which you have in Christ Jesus and the love which you show towards all God's people while you look forward to the hope which is stored up for you in heaven as a treasure for the life to come. This hope was communicated to you in those earlier lessons, when the Gospel was preached to you in its purity and integrity—the one universal unchangeable Gospel which was made known to you, even as it was carried throughout the world, approving itself by its fruits wherever it is planted. For, as elsewhere, so also in you, these fruits were manifested from the first day when you received your lessons in, and apprehended the power of, the genuine Gospel, which is not a law of ordinances but a dispensation of grace, not a device of men but a truth of God. Such was the word preached to you by Epaphras, our beloved fellow servant in our Master's household, who in our absence and on our behalf has ministered to you the Gospel of Christ and who now brings back to us the welcome tidings of the love which you show in the Spirit.

3. Father. If the word "and" is omitted, as the balance of the authorities appears to suggest, the form of words here is quite exceptional. Elsewhere it runs, "the God and Father of our Lord Jesus Christ" (see Romans 15:6; 2 Corinthians 1:3; 11:31; Ephesians 1:3; 1 Peter 1:3; compare Revelation 1:6). In Colossians 3:17 we have the words "God the Father," which is also an unusual expression.

Always. We here meet the same difficulty about the link between clauses which confronts us in several of St. Paul's opening thanksgivings. The words **always** and **for you** would be inexplicable if they came at the beginning of a clause. But are they to be linked to the preceding or the following sentence? The connection with the previous words is favored by St. Paul's usual conjunction of "always thank" and by the parallel passage in Ephesians 1:16. Thus the words will mean, "We give thanks for you always in our prayers." For this absolute use of **when we pray** see Matthew 6:7 and Acts 16:25.

4. We have heard. "Having heard" from Epaphras (verse 8), for the apostle had no direct personal knowledge of the Colossian church.

In Christ Jesus. This links with **your faith.** The strict classical language would require "*the* faith in Christ." But the omission of the article is common in the New Testament (for example, verse 8, which in the Greek only has the words "in Spirit"). The preposition **in** here and in the parallel passage, Ephesians 1:15, denotes the sphere in which their faith moves, rather than the object to which it is directed (compare 1 Corinthians 3:5).

5. The faith. "For the hope," that is, looking to the hope. The hope here is identified with the object of the hope. The sense of **hope,** as with the corresponding words in any language, oscillates between the subjective feeling and the objective realization; compare Romans 8:24, "For in this hope we were saved. But hope that is seen is no hope at all. Who hopes for what he already has?," where it passes abruptly from the one to the other.

That is stored up. This is the word used in the Gospels; see Matthew 6:20-21; Luke 12:34; 18:22.

That you have already heard about. "Of which you were told in time past." This seems intended to contrast their earlier and latter lessons—the true Gospel of Epaphras with the false gospel of their recent teachers.

The word of truth, the gospel. "The truth of the Gospel," that is, the true and genuine Gospel as taught by Epaphras, and not the spurious substitute of these later pretenders (compare verse 6, **its truth**). See also Galatians 2:5, 14, where a similar contrast is implied in the use of "the truth of the gospel."

6. All over the world. For a similar hyperbole see Romans 1:8, and compare 1 Thessalonians 1:8 and 2 Corinthians 2:14. More is hidden under these words than appears on the surface. The true Gospel, the apostle seems to say, proclaims its truth by its universality. The false gospels are the outgrowths of local circumstances, of special idiosyncrasies; the true Gospel is the same everywhere. The false gospels address themselves to limited circles; the true Gospel proclaims itself boldly throughout the world. Heresies are at best ethnic; truth is essentially universal. (See verse 23.)

Is bearing fruit. "Is constantly bearing fruit." The fruit which the Gospel bears without fail in all soils and under every climate is its credential, its verification, as against the pretensions of spurious counterfeits. The substantive verb should here be taken with the participle to express the continuity of the present action, as in 2 Corinthians 9:12 and Philippians 2:26. It is less common in St. Paul than in some of the canonical writers, such as Mark and Luke, but probably only because he deals less in narrative.

Of the middle **bearing fruit** no other instance has been found. The use of the middle points to the force of the word here. The middle is intensive, the active extensive. The middle denotes the inherent energy, the active, the external diffusion. The Gospel is essentially a reproductive organism, a plant whose seed is in itself.

And growing. The Gospel is not like those plants which exhaust themselves in bearing fruit and wither away. The external growth keeps pace with the reproductive energy. While bearing fruit describes the inner working, growing gives the outer extension of the Gospel. The words and growing are not found in the received text, but the authority in their favor is overwhelming.

God's grace. St. Paul's synonym for the Gospel. In Acts 20:24 he says it is his mission to preach "the gospel of God's grace." The true Gospel as taught by Epaphras was an offer of free grace, a message from God; the false gospel, as imposed by the heretical teachers, was a code of rigorous prohibitions, a system of human devising. It was not **grace** but **regulations**" (see 2:14); not "of God," but **of this world** (see 2:8, 20, 22). For God's power and goodness it substituted self-mortification and self-exaltation. The Gospel is called God's grace again in 2 Corinthians 6:1 and 8:9, with reference to the same leading characteristic which the apostle delights to dwell on (see Romans 3:24; 5:15; Ephesians 2:5, 8) and which he here tacitly contrasts with the teachings of the later intruders. The false teachers of Colosse, like those of Galatia, would "set aside the grace of God" (Galatians 2:21); to accept their doctrine was to "have fallen away from grace" (Galatians 5:4).

In all its truth. "In its genuine simplicity, without adulteration."

7. You learned it. "Even as you were instructed in it"—the clause explains the preceding **in all its truth.**

Epaphras. On his work as the evangelist of the Colossians, see the note on 4:12.

Fellow servant. See 4:7. The word does not occur elsewhere in St. Paul.

8. And who also told. "As he preached to you from us, so also he brought back to us from you the tidings, etc."

In the Spirit. This is linked with **your love.** "The fruit of the Spirit is love" (Galatians 5:22). For the omission of the article from **in the Spirit** see notes on verse 4.

Prayer for Their Future Advance in Knowledge and Well-doing Through Christ (1:9-14)

For this reason, since the day we heard about you, we have not stopped praying for you and asking God to fill you with the knowledge of his will through all spiritual wisdom and understanding. And we pray this in order that you may live a life worthy of the Lord and may please him in every way: bearing fruit in every good work, growing in the knowledge of God, being strengthened with all power according to his glorious might so that you may have great endurance and patience, and joyfully giving thanks to the Father, who has qualified you to share in the inheritance of the saints in the kingdom of light. For he has rescued us from the dominion of darkness and brought us into the kingdom of the Son he loves, in whom we have redemption, the forgiveness of sins.

Hearing then that you thus abound in works of faith and love, we on our part have not ceased, from the day when we received the happy tidings, to pray on your behalf. And this is the purport of our petitions; that you may grow more and more in knowledge, until you attain to the perfect understanding of God's will, being endowed with all wisdom to apprehend his verities and all intelligence to follow his processes, living in the mind of the Spirit—to the end that knowledge may manifest itself in practice, that your conduct in life may be worthy of your profession in the Lord, so as in all ways to win for you the gracious favor of God your King. Thus, while you bear fruit in every good work, you will also grow as the tree grows, being watered and refreshed by this knowledge, as by the dew of heaven: thus you will be strengthened in all strength, according to that power which enters in and spreads from his glorious manifestation of himself, and nerved to all endurance under affliction and all long-suffering under provocation, not only without complaining, but even with joy: thus finally (for this is the crown of all), so rejoicing you will pour out your thanksgiving to the universal Father, who prepared and fitted us all—you and us alike—to take possession of the portion which his goodness has allotted to us among the saints in the kingdom of his light. Yes, by a strong arm he rescued us from the lawless tyranny of darkness, removed us from the land of our bondage, and settled us as free citizens in our new and glorious home, where his Son, the offspring and the representative of his love, is King; even the same who paid our ransom and thus procured our redemption from captivity—our redemption, which (be assured) is nothing else than the remission of our sins.

9. For this reason. That is, "by reason of your progressive faith and love." **The knowledge.** A favorite word in the later letters of St. Paul. In all four letters of the first Roman captivity, it is an element in the apostle's opening prayer for his correspondents' well-being (Philippians 1:9; Ephesians 1:17; Philemon 6; and here). The greater stress which is thus laid on the contemplative aspects of the Gospel may be explained partly by St. Paul's personal circumstances and partly by the requirements of the church. His enforced inactivity and comparative leisure would lead his own thoughts in this direction, while at the same time the fresh dangers threatening the truth from the side of mystic speculation required confrontation by an exposition of the Gospel from a corresponding point of view.

The compound translated **knowledge** (literally "full knowledge") is used especially of the knowledge of God and of Christ as the perfection of knowledge (see Proverbs 2:5; Hosea 4:1; 6:6; Ephesians 1:17; 4:13; 2 Peter 1:2, 8; 2:20).

Wisdom and understanding. These two words are frequently found together (see Exodus 31:3 [KJV]; Deuteronomy 4:6; 1 Chronicles 22:12; 2 Chronicles 1:10; Isaiah 11:2; 29:14 [KJV]; Daniel 2:20; 1 Corinthians 1:19 [KJV]).

Spiritual. The word is emphatic from its position in the Greek (where it is the last word in the sentence). The false teachers also offered a **wisdom**, but it had only a show of wisdom (see 2:23); it was an empty counterfeit calling itself philosophy (2:8); it was the offspring of vanity nurtured by the unspiritual mind (2:18). (Also see 2 Corinthians 1:12, where a similar contrast is implied, and 1 Corinthians 1:20; 2:5-6, 13; 3:19, where it is directly expressed.)

10. Live a life worthy. See 1 Thessalonians 2:12 and Ephesians 4:1, and compare Philippians 1:27. The infinitive here denotes the consequence of the spiritual enlightenment of being filled with **the knowledge of [God's] will.**

Please. That is, "to please God in all ways"; compare 1 Thessalonians 4:1. As this word for **please** was commonly used to describe the correct attitude of men toward God, the addition of "God" would not be necessary.

In every. That is, "not only showing the fruits of your faith before men (Matthew 5:16), but yourselves growing meanwhile in moral stature (Ephesians 4:13)."

The knowledge of God. The simple instrumental dative represents the knowledge of God as the dew or the rain which nurtures the growth of the plant (see Deuteronomy 32:2; Hosea 14:5).

11. Being strengthened. This word is not found elsewhere in the New Testament, except in Hebrews 11:34.

According to his . . . might. The power communicated to the faithful corresponds to, and is a function of, the divine might from which it comes. Unlike other words for might or power used in the New Testament, such as *dunamis* or *ischus*, the Greek word here used for **might**, *kratos*, is applied solely to God in the New Testament.

Glorious. The glory here, as often elsewhere, stands for the majesty or the power or the goodness of God, as manifested to men (see Ephesians 1:6, 12, 17; 3:16; compare Colossians 1:27). The glory (*doxa*), the bright light over the mercy-seat (Romans 9:4), was a symbol of such manifestations. God's revelation of himself to us, however this revelation may be made, is the one source of all our highest strength.

Endurance and patience. The two words occur in the same context in 2 Corinthians 6:4, 6; 2 Timothy 3:10; James 5:10-11. The difference between their meanings is best seen in their opposites. While **endurance** or perseverance is the temper which does not easily succumb under suffering, **patience** is the self-restraint which does not hastily retaliate a wrong. The one is opposed to cowardice or despondency, the other to wrath or revenge (see Proverbs 15:18; 16:32). While 'endurance is closely allied to hope (1 Thessalonians 1:3), **patience** is often connected with mercy (Exodus 34:6).

Joyfully. See James 1:2-3 and compare 1 Peter 4:13, and see below on 1:24. The parallel in James points to the correct link of **joyfully** with the preceding words.

12. Giving thanks. This is most naturally linked with the preceding participles and refers to the Colossians. The duty of thanksgiving is more than once laid on them later in this letter (2:7; 3:15-17; 4:2: compare 1 Thessalonians 5:18.)

Who has qualified you (some manuscripts: **us**). Compare 2 Corinthians 3:6.

To share in the inheritance. "The portion which consists in the lot." The inheritance of Canaan, the allotment of the promised land, here presents an analogy to, and supplies a metaphor for, the higher hopes of the new dispensation, as in Hebrews 3:7—4:11. This is not won by us but is allotted to us.

Light. The **inheritance of the saints** is situated in **the kingdom of light**. For the whole context compare St. Paul's narrative in Acts 26:18, where all these ideas and many of these expressions recur. See also Acts 20:32, another of St. Paul's later speeches.

13. "We were slaves in the land of darkness. God rescued us from this thralldom. He transplanted us from there and settled us as free colonists and citizens in the kingdom of his Son, in the realms of light."

Rescued. "Rescued, delivered us" by his strong arm, as a mighty conqueror; compare 2:15, **triumphing**.

Dominion. "Arbitrary power, tyranny." The word "authority" correctly signifies "liberty of action" and, like the corresponding English word "license," involves two secondary ideas, of which either may be so prominent as to eclipse the other: firstly "authority," "delegated power" (see Luke 20:2) or, secondly, "tyranny," "lawlessness," "unrestrained or arbitrary power." This latter idea of a capricious, unruly rule is prominent here. This expression **dominion of darkness** occurs in Luke 22:53, where the idea of disorder is involved. The transference from darkness to light is here represented as a transference from an arbitrary tyranny, a **dominion**, to a well-ordered sovereignty, a **kingdom**.

Brought us. "Removed" when they accepted Christ. The image of **brought us** is supplied by the wholesale transportation of peoples, of which the history of oriental monarchies supplied so many examples.

Of the Son. Not of inferior angels, as the false teachers would have it (2:18), but of his own Son. The same contrast between a dispensation of angels and a dispensation of the Son underlies the words here and is explicitly brought out in Hebrews 1:1—2:8; see especially Hebrews 1:2, compared with Hebrews 1:5.

He loves. "Of his love." As love is the essence of the Father (1 John 4:8, 16), so it is also of the Son. The mission of the Son is the revelation of the Father's love.

In the preceding verses we have a striking illustration of St. Paul's teaching in two important respects. First, Christ's reign has already begun. His kingdom is a present kingdom. Whatever therefore is essential in Christ's kingdom must be capable of realization now. There may be some exceptional manifestation in the world to come, but this cannot alter its inherent character. In other words, the sovereignty of Christ is essentially a moral and spiritual sovereignty which has begun now and will only be perfected hereafter.

Second, and corresponding to this and equally significant, is St. Paul's language in speaking about individual Christians. He regards them as already rescued from the power of darkness, as already put in possession of their inheritance as saints. They are potentially saved because the knowledge of God is itself salvation, and this knowledge is within their reach. Such is St. Paul's constant way of speaking. He uses the language not of exclusion but of comprehension. He prefers to dwell on their potential advantages rather than on their actual attainments. He hopes to make them saints by dwelling on their calling as saints. See especially Ephesians 2:6.

14. Redemption (a few late manuscripts: **Redemption through his blood**). The image of a captive and enslaved people is continued. The metaphor, however, has changed from the victor who rescues the captive by force of arms—**rescued** (verse 13)—to the philanthropist who releases him by the payment of a ransom.

The forgiveness of sins. In the parallel passage in Ephesians 1:7, the apostle defines redemption as the forgiveness of sins.

Colossians 1:15—2:3

The Preeminence of the Son (1:15-19)

In the passage which follows, St. Paul defines the Person of Christ, claiming for him absolute supremacy: first, in relation to the universe, the natural creation (verses 15-17); second, in relation to the church, the new moral creation (verse 18). He then combines the two, explaining this twofold sovereignty by the absolute indwelling of the *pleroma* in Christ and showing how, as a consequence, the reconciliation and harmony of all things must be effected in him (verse 19; compare verse 20).

As the idea of the *Logos* underlies the whole of this passage, though the term itself does not appear, a few words to explain this term are necessary by way of preface. The word *logos*, denoting both "reason" and "speech," was a philosophical term adopted by Alexandrian Judaism before St. Paul wrote, to express the manifestation of the Unseen God, the Absolute Being, in the creation and government of the world. It included all modes by which God makes himself known to man. As his reason, it denoted his purpose or design; as his speech, it implied his revelation.

Christian teachers, when they adopted this term, exalted and fixed its meaning by attaching to it two precise and definite ideas: first, the Word is a divine person (John 1:1); and, second, the Word became incarnate in Jesus Christ (John 1:14). It is obvious that these two propositions must have altered materially the significance of all the subordinate terms connected with the idea of the *logos*, and that therefore their use in Alexandrian writers, such as Philo, cannot be taken to define, though it may be brought to illustrate, their meaning in St. Paul and St. John. With these cautions the Alexandrian phraseology, as a providential preparation for the teaching of

71

the Gospel, will afford important aid in the understanding of the apostolic writings.

15-19. He is the image of the invisible God, the firstborn over all creation. For by him all things were created: things in heaven and on earth, visible and invisible, whether thrones or powers or rulers or authorities; all things were created by him and for him. He is before all things, and in him all things hold together. And he is the head of the body, the church; he is the beginning and the firstborn from among the dead, so that in everything he might have the supremacy. For God was pleased to have all his fullness dwell in him.

15-17. He is the perfect image, the visible representation, of the unseen God. He is the Firstborn, the absolute Heir of the Father, begotten before the ages; the Lord of the universe by virtue of primogeniture, and by virtue also of creative agency. For in and through him the whole world was created, things in heaven and things on earth, things visible to the outward eye and things cognizable by the inward perception. His supremacy is absolute and universal. All powers in heaven and earth are subject to him. This subjection extends even to the most exalted and most potent of angelic beings, whether they are called thrones or dominations or princedoms or powers, or whatever title of dignity men may confer on them. Yes: he is the first and he is the last. Through him, as the mediatorial Word, the universe has been created; and unto him, as the final goal, it is tending. In him is no before or after. He is preexistent and self-existent before all the worlds. And in him, as the binding and sustaining power, universal nature coheres and consists.

15. He is the image of the invisible God, the firstborn over all creation. The person of Christ is described first especially in relation to deity, as **the image of the invisible God,** and second, especially in relation to created things, as **the firstborn over all creation.** The fundamental idea of the *Logos* involves the idea of mediation between God and creation. A perverted view about the nature of the mediation between the two lay at the root of the heretical teaching at Colosse and had to be met by the true teaching of Christ as the eternal *Logos.*

The image. This expression is used repeatedly by Philo as a description of the *Logos.* St. Paul applies the term to our Lord in an earlier letter, 2 Corinthians 4:4: "the glory of Christ, who is the image of God"; compare 2 Corinthians 3:18.

Beyond the very obvious notion of likeness, the word **image** involves two other ideas.

First, representation. **Image** implies the archetype of which it is a copy. The **image** might be the result of direct imitation like the head of a sovereign on a coin, or it might be due to natural causes like the parental features in the child, but in any case it was derived from its prototype. The word itself, however, does not necessarily imply perfect representation. Thus man is said to be the image of God (1 Corinthians 11:7).

Second, manifestation. The underlying idea of **image** is the manifestation of the hidden. The Word, whether preincarnate or incarnate, is the revelation of the unseen Father (compare John 1:18; 14:9-10).

The firstborn over all creation. The word **firstborn** has a twofold parentage.

First, like **image**, it is closely connected with and taken from the Alexandrian vocabulary of the *Logos*. Among the early Christian fathers Justin Martyr again and again recognizes the application of the term **firstborn** to the Word.

Second, the word **firstborn** had another important link with the past. The messianic reference of Psalm 89:27—"I will also appoint him my firstborn"—seems to have been generally allowed. So at least it is interpreted by R. Nathan: "God said, 'As I made Jacob a first-born (Exodus 4:22), so also will I make king Messiah a first-born (Psalm 89:27).'" Hence **the firstborn**, used absolutely, became a recognized title of the Messiah.

As the person of Christ was the divine response both to the philosophical questionings of the Alexandrian Jew and to the patriotic hopes of the Palestinian, those two currents of thought met in the term **firstborn** as applied to our Lord, who is both the true *Logos* and the true Messiah. The main ideas then which the word **firstborn** involves are twofold: the one more directly linked with the Alexandrian conception of the *Logos*, the other more closely allied to the Palestinian conception of the Messiah.

First, priority to all creation. In other words it declares the absolute preexistence of the Son.

Second, sovereignty over all creation. God's **firstborn** is the natural ruler, the acknowledged head, of God's household.

Over all creation. "All creation" rather than "every created thing." The three senses of "creation" in the New Testament are, first, creation as the action of creating (Romans 1:20); second, creation as the aggregate of created things (Mark 13:19, KJV; Romans 8:22); third, a creation, a single created thing, a creature (Romans 8:39, KJV; Hebrews 4:13, KJV). As **creation** without the definite article is sometimes used of the created world generally (Mark 13:19, KJV), it is best taken so here.

The genitive case must be interpreted to include the full meaning of **firstborn**. It will therefore signify: "He stands in the relation of 'firstborn' to all creation"; that is, "He is the Firstborn and, as the Firstborn, the absolute heir and sovereign Lord of all creation."

16. For by him all things were created. We have in this sentence the justification of the title given to the Son in the preceding clause, **firstborn over**

all creation. It must therefore be taken to explain the sense in which this title is used. Thus linked, it shows that the **firstborn** himself is not included in **all creation**.

For by him. Compare with verse 17. For the preposition compare with Acts 17:28. All the laws and purposes which guide the creation and government of the universe reside in him, the eternal Word, as their meeting-point. The apostolic doctrine of the *Logos* teaches us to regard the eternal Word as having the same relation to the universe which the incarnate Christ holds to the church. He is the source of its life, the center of all its developments, the mainspring of all its motions. The use of this preposition **by** (literally "in") to describe his relationship to the church abounds in St. Paul (Romans 8:1-2; 12:5; 16:3, 7, 9; 1 Corinthians 1:30; 4:15, 17; 7:39 [KJV]; 15:18, 22), and more especially in the letters to the Colossians (2:7, 10) and Ephesians. In the present passage, as in Colossians 1:17, the same preposition is applied to the universe (compare John 1:4).

Were created. The aorist tense is used here, which describes the definite historical act of creation.

All things. "The universe of things"; not "all things severally," but "all things collectively." With very few exceptions, wherever this phrase occurs elsewhere, it stands in a similar connection (Colossians 1:17, 20; 3:11; Romans 11:36; 1 Corinthians 8:6; 11:12; 12:6; 15:27-28; 2 Corinthians 5:18; Ephesians 1:10-11, 23; 4:10; Hebrews 1:3; 2:8; Revelation 4:11). Thus it is seen that **all things** is almost equivalent to "the universe."

Things in heaven and on earth. This division of the universe should be compared with Genesis 1:1, 2:1, 14:19, and Revelation 10:6.

Whether thrones or powers or rulers or authorities. The apostle singles out those created beings that from their superior rank had been or might try to rival the Son.

A comparison with the parallel passage in Ephesians 1:21 brings out the following points.

First, no stress can be laid on the sequence of the names, as though St. Paul were enunciating with authority some precise doctrine about the grades of celestial hierarchy. The names themselves are not the same in the two passages. While "rulers," "authorities," and "powers" are common to both, **thrones** is peculiar to one and "dominion" to the other. Nor again is there any correspondence in the sequence. Neither does "dominion" take the place of **thrones**, nor do the three words common to both appear in the same order.

Second, an expression in Ephesians 1:21 shows the apostle's motive for introducing these lists of names, for he adds, "and every title that can be given, not only in the present age but also in the one to come," that is, "of every dignity or title (whether real or imaginary) which is reverenced." Hence it appears that in this catalog St. Paul does not profess to describe objective realities but contents himself with repeating subjective opinions.

He brushes away all these speculations without inquiring how much or how little truth there may be in them, because they are altogether beside the question. His language here shows the same spirit of impatience with this elaborate angelology as in 2:18.

Third, some commentators have referred the terms used here solely to earthly potentates and dignities. There can be little doubt, however, that their chief and primary reference is to the orders of the celestial hierarchy, as conceived by these Gnostic Judaizers. The whole design and purport of the letter points to this, as it was written to combat the worship given to angels. The names too, especially **thrones**, are linked with the speculations of Jewish angelology. But when this is granted, two questions still remain. First, are evil as well as good spirits included, demons as well as angels? And next, though the primary reference is to spiritual powers, is it not possible that the expression was intended to be comprehensive and to include earthly dignitaries as well? The clause added in the parallel passage, "not only in the present age but also in the one to come" (Ephesians 1:21) encourages us to extend the apostle's meaning in this way. We are also led in the same direction by the comprehensive words which have preceded here, **things in heaven and on earth.** Nor is there anything in the terms themselves which bars such an extension, for the combination of **rulers** and **authorities** is applied not only to good angels but to bad, not only to spiritual powers but to earthly.

Thus guided, we may paraphrase the apostle's meaning as follows: "You dispute much about the successive grades of angels; you distinguish each grade by its special title; you can tell how each order was generated from the preceding; you assign to each its proper degree of worship. Meanwhile, you have ignored or you have degraded Christ. I tell you, it is not so. He is first and foremost Lord of heaven and earth, far above all thrones and dominations, all princedoms or powers, far above every dignitary and every potentate—whether earthly or heavenly—whether angel or demon or man—that evokes your reverence or excites your fear."

Thrones belonged to the highest grade of angelic beings, whose place is in the immediate presence of God. The meaning of the name, however, is doubtful. First, it may signify the occupants of thrones which surround the throne of God, as in the imagery of Revelation 4:4. The imagery there is taken from the court of an earthly king (see Jeremiah 52:32). Second, it seems best to treat **thrones** as belonging to the same category as **powers or rulers or authorities,** which are concrete words borrowed from different grades of human rank and power. As implying regal dignity, **thrones** naturally stands at the head of the list.

Powers. See Ephesians 1:21, "dominion." These appear to have been regarded as belonging to the first grade, standing next in order to **thrones.** This indeed would be suggested by their name.

Rulers or authorities. As in Ephesians 1:21. These two words occur very frequently together. In some places they refer to human dignities (Luke 12:11; Titus 3:1), in others to a spiritual hierarchy. And here again there are two different uses: sometimes they designate good angels (2:10; Ephesians 3:10), sometimes evil spirits (2:15; Ephesians 6:12), while in one passage at least (1 Corinthians 15:24) both may be included.

All things were created by him and for him. "As all creation passed out from him, so does it all converge again toward him." He is not only the Alpha but also the Omega, not only the beginning but the end of creation, not only the first but also the last in the history of the universe (Revelation 22:13). For this double relation of Christ to the universe, as both the initial and the final cause, see Hebrews 2:10.

For him. As of the Father it is said elsewhere (1 Corinthians 8:6), so here of the Son we read, **all things were created by him and for him**. All things must find their meeting-point, their reconciliation, at length in him from whom they took their rise—in the Word as the mediatorial agent, and through the Word in the Father as the primary source. The Word is the final cause as well as the creative agent of the universe. This ultimate goal of the present dispensation in time is similarly stated in several passages. Sometimes it is represented as the birth-throe and deliverance of all creation through Christ (Romans 8:19). Sometimes it is the absolute and final subjection of the universal nature to him (1 Corinthians 15:28). Sometimes it is the reconciliation of all things through him (Colossians 1:20). Sometimes it is the recapitulation, the gathering up in one head, of the universe in him (Ephesians 1:10). The image in this last reference best illustrates the particular expression in the text **created . . . for him**; but each of them enunciates the same truth in different ways. The eternal Word is the goal of the universe, just as he was the starting point. It must end in unity, just as it proceeded from unity: and the center of that unity is Christ.

17. He is before all things. Compare John 8:58. The imperfect tense might have sufficed, but the present **is** declares that this preexistence is absolute existence. The **he** is as necessary for the completeness of the meaning as the **is**. The one emphasized the personality; the other declares the preexistence. For this emphatic **he** see again verse 18 (compare Ephesians 2:14; 4:10-11; 1 John 2:2; and especially Revelation 19:15).

All things hold together. "Cohere." He is the principle of cohesion in the universe. He impresses on creation that unity and solidarity which makes it a cosmos instead of a chaos. Thus, to take one instance, the action of gravity, which keeps things fixed in their places and regulates the movement of things, is an expression of Christ's mind. Similarly in Hebrews 1:3, Christ, the *Logos*, is described "as sustaining all things," that is, sustaining the universe.

18. And not only does he hold this position of absolute priority and sovereignty over the universe—the natural creation—but he stands in the same relationship to the church—the new spiritual creation. He is its head, and it is his body. That is his prerogative, because he is the source and the beginning of its life, being **the firstborn from among the dead**. Thus in all things—in the spiritual order as in the natural, in the church as in the world—he is found to have the preeminence.

And he. This is repeated from the previous verse to emphasize the identity of the person who unites in himself these prerogatives; see the comments on verse 17. The Creator of the world is also the Head of the church. There is no blind ignorance, no imperfect sympathy, no latent conflict in the relationship between the Creator of the world and the dispensation of the Gospel, as the heretical teachers were disposed consciously or unconsciously to assume, but rather an absolute unity of origin.

The head. The inspiring, ruling, guiding, combining, sustaining power, the mainspring of its activity, the center of its unity, and the seat of its life. In Paul's earlier letters the relationship of the church to Christ is described in the same way (1 Corinthians 12:12-27; compare Romans 12:4). The apostle there takes as his starting-point the various functions of the members, and also the originating and controlling power of the Head. Compare 1:24; 2:19; Ephesians 1:22; 2:16; 4:4, 12, 15; 5:23, 30.

The church. This is in apposition with **the body**; compare 1:24; Ephesians 1:23.

He is the beginning. "The origin." The term is here applied to the incarnate Christ in his relationship to the church because it is applicable to the eternal Word in relationship to the universe (Revelation 3:14). The parallelism of the two relationships is kept in view throughout. The word **beginning** here involves two ideas. First, priority in time. Christ was the first-fruits of the dead (1 Corinthians 15:20, 23). Second, originating power. Christ was also the source of life (Acts 3:15; Hebrews 2:10). He rose first from the dead, that others might rise through him.

Firstborn. Compare Revelation 1:5. Christ's resurrection from the dead is his title to the headship of the church, for "the power of his resurrection" (Philippians 3:10) is the life of the church. The words **firstborn from among the dead** here correspond to **firstborn over all creation** in verse 15, so that the parallelism between Christ's relationship to the universe and to the church is thus emphasized.

So that in everything . . .. As Christ is first with respect to the universe, so it was ordained that he **might have the supremacy** with respect to the church as well. The **might have** here answers in a manner to the **is** of verse 17. Thus the **is** and **might have** are contrasted as the absolute being and the historical manifestation. The relationship between Christ's headship of the universe by virtue of his eternal Godhead and his headship of the church by virtue of his incarnation and passion and resurrection is somewhat similarly represented in Philippians 2:6.

77

In everything. Not in the universe only, but in the church also.

19. And this absolute supremacy is his because it was the Father's good pleasure that in him all the plenitude of deity should have its home.

For . . . in him. The eternal indwelling of the Godhead explains the headship of the church no less than the headship of the universe. The resurrection of Christ, whereby he became the **beginning** of the church, was the result of and the testimony to his deity (Romans 1:4).

All his fullness. "The plenitude" (Greek: *pleroma*), a recognized technical term in theology, denoting the totality of the divine powers and attributes; compare 2:9. See earlier note on *pleroma*.

Dwell. "Should have its permanent abode." The word occurs again in the same context at 2:9. The false teachers probably, like their later counterparts, maintained only a partial and transient connection of *pleroma* with the Lord.

The Work of the Son—
A Work of Reconciliation (1:20—2:3)

> **20. . . . and through him to reconcile to himself all things, whether things on earth or things in heaven, by making peace through his blood, shed on the cross.**

> *. . . because he willed through him to reconcile the universe once more to himself. It was God's purpose to effect peace and harmony through the blood of Christ's cross, and so to restore all things, whatsoever and wheresoever they be, whether on the earth or in the heavens.*

20. The false teachers aimed at effecting a partial reconciliation between God and man through the interposition of angelic mediators. The apostle speaks of an absolute and complete reconciliation of universal nature to God, effected through the mediation of the incarnate Word. Their mediators were ineffective, because they were neither human nor divine. The true mediator must be both human and divine. It was necessary that in him all the plenitude of the Godhead should dwell. It was necessary also that he should be born into the world and should suffer as a man.

Through him. That is, "through Christ," as is clear from the **in him** of the previous verse. The expression **through him** has already been applied to the preincarnate Word in relation to the universe (verse 16); it is now used of the incarnate Word in relation to the church.

To reconcile. The corresponding word used in Ephesians 2:16 implies a restitution to a state from which they had fallen, or which was potentially theirs, or for which they were destined.

All things. The whole universe of things, material as well as spiritual, will be restored to harmony with God. How far this restoration of universal nature may be subjective, as involved in the changed perceptions of man thus brought into harmony with God, and how far it may have an objective and independent existence, it was vain to speculate.

To himself. The reconciliation is always represented as made to the Father. The reconciler is sometimes the Father (2 Corinthians 5:18-19), sometimes the Son (Ephesians 2:16; compare Romans 5:10-11).

21-23. Once you were alienated from God and were enemies in your minds because of your evil behavior. But now he has reconciled you by Christ's physical body through death to present you holy in his sight, without blemish and free from accusation—if you continue in your faith, established and firm, not moved from the hope held out in the gospel. This is the gospel that you heard and that has been proclaimed to every creature under heaven, and of which I, Paul, have become a servant.

And you too—you Gentiles—are included in the terms of this peace. In times past you had estranged yourselves from God. Your hearts were hostile to him while you lived on in your evil deeds. But now, in Christ's body, in Christ's flesh which died on the cross for your atonement, you are reconciled to him again. He will present you a living sacrifice, an acceptable offering to himself, free from blemish and free even from censure, that you may stand the piercing glance of him whose scrutiny no defect can escape. But this can only be if you remain true to your old allegiance, if you hold fast (as I trust you are holding fast) by the teaching of Epaphras, if the edifice of your faith is built on solid foundations and not reared carelessly on the sands, if you suffer not yourselves to be shifted or shaken but rest firmly on the hope which you have found in the Gospel— the one universal unchangeable Gospel which was proclaimed to every creature under heaven, of which I Paul, unworthy as I am, was called to be a minister.

21. Alienated. "Estranged," not strangers; compare Ephesians 2:12; 4:18.

Enemies. "Hostile" to God, as the consequence of being "estranged," not "hateful to God," as it is taken by some. The active rather than the passive sense of "enemies" is required by the context, which (as commonly in the New Testament) speaks of the sinner as reconciled to God, not of God as reconciled to the sinner; compare Romans 5:10. It is the mind of man, not the mind of God, which must undergo a change, so a reunion may be effected.

In your minds. "In your mind, your intent." For the dative of the part affected, compare Ephesians 4:18; Luke 1:51.

22. But now. Here, as frequently, **now** admits an aorist because it denotes not "at the present moment" but in the present dispensation, the present order of things; compare verse 26; Romans 5:11; 7:6; 11:30-31; 16:26; Ephesians 2:13; 3:5; 2 Timothy 1:10; 1 Peter 1:8; 2:10, 25. In all these passages there is a direct contrast between the old dispensation and the new, especially as affecting the relation of the Gentiles to God.

By Christ's physical body (Greek, "of his body"). It has been suggested that St. Paul added these words, which are evidently emphatic, with a polemical aim—either to combat docetism (of this form of error, however, there is no direct evidence until a somewhat later date) or to combat false spiritualism which took offense at the teaching of an atoning sacrifice. But for this purpose they would not have been adequate, because not explicit enough. It seems simpler, therefore, to suppose that they were added for the sake of greater clarity, to distinguish the natural body of Christ intended here from the mystical body mentioned just above, in verse 18.

To present. This is said of God himself, as in 2 Corinthians 4:14.

Without blemish. Rather than "without blame." It is a sacrificial word.

Free from accusation. This is an advance on **without blemish**—"in whom not only no blemish is found, but against whom no charge is brought"; compare 1 Timothy 6:14. The Greek word translated **free from accusation** occurs also in 1 Corinthians 1:8, 1 Timothy 3:10, Titus 1:6-7.

In his sight. Does this refer to God's future judgment or his present approbation? The latter seems more probable as it has this meaning in the parallel passage in Ephesians 1:4. Where the future judgment is intended, a different expression is found (see 2 Corinthians 5:10).

23. If. This expresses a pure hypothesis in itself, but the indicative mood following converts the hypothesis into a hope.

Established and firm. "Built on a foundation and so firm"; not like the house of the foolish man in the parable who built "without a foundation" (Luke 6:49). For **established** compare Ephesians 3:17.

To every creature. In fulfillment of the Lord's last command (see Mark 16:15). The expression **to every creature** must not be limited to man. The statement is given in the broadest form, all creation, animate and inanimate, being included, as in Revelation 5:13. For the hyperbole **to every creature**, compare 1 Thessalonians 1:8. To demand statistical exactness in such a context would be to require what is never required in similar cases. The apostle's motive here is to emphasize the universality of the genuine Gospel, which has been offered without reserve to all alike, and to appeal to its public presence as the credential and guarantee of its truth.

And of which I, Paul, have become a servant. Why does St. Paul introduce himself here so abruptly? His motive can hardly be the assertion of his apostolic authority, for it does not appear that this was questioned; otherwise he would have declared his commission in stronger terms. We can only answer that impressed with the dignity of his office, as involving the offer of grace to the Gentiles, he cannot refrain from magnifying it. At the same time this mention enables him to link himself in ties of closer sympathy with the Colossians, and he passes on at once to his relationship with them; compare Ephesians 3:2-9; 1 Timothy 1:11, in which latter passage the introduction of his own name is equally abrupt.

I, Paul. "Weak and unworthy as I am"; compare Ephesians 3:8.

24-27. Now I rejoice in what was suffered for you, and I fill up in my flesh what is still lacking in regard to Christ's afflictions, for the sake of his body, which is the church. I have become its servant by the commission God gave me to present to you the word of God in its fullness—the mystery that has been kept hidden for ages and generations, but is now disclosed to the saints. To them God has chosen to make known among the Gentiles the glorious riches of this mystery, which is Christ in you, the hope of glory.

Now when I see the full extent of God's mercy, now when I ponder over his mighty work of reconciliation, I cannot choose but rejoice in my sufferings. Yes, I Paul the persecutor, I Paul the feeble and sinful, am permitted to supplement—I do not shrink from the word—to supplement the afflictions of Christ. Despite all that he underwent, the Master has left something for me the servant to undergo. And so my flesh is privileged to suffer for his body—his spiritual body, the church. I was appointed a minister of the church, a steward in God's household, for this very purpose, that I might administer my office on your behalf, might dispense to you Gentiles the stores which his bountiful grace has provided. Thus I was charged to preach without reserve the whole Gospel of God, to proclaim the great mystery which had remained a secret through all the ages and all the generations, but which now in these last times was revealed to his holy people. For such was his good pleasure. God willed to make known to them, in all its inexhaustible wealth thus displayed through the call of the Gentiles, the glorious revelation of this mystery—Christ not the Saviour of the Jews only, but Christ dwelling in you, Christ become to you the hope of glory.

24. Now I rejoice. A sudden outburst of thanksgiving, that he who was less than the least, who was not worthy to be called an apostle, should be allowed to share and even to supplement the sufferings of Christ.

The thought underlying **now** seems to be this: "If ever I have been disposed to repine at my lot, if ever I have felt my cross almost too heavy to bear, yet now—now, when I contemplate the lavish wealth of God's mercy—now when I see all the glory of bearing a part in this magnificent work—my sorrow is turned to joy."

I fill up in my flesh. Single compounds of this verb (1 Corinthians 14:16 [KJV]; 16:17; Galatians 6:2) and double compounds of this verb

(2 Corinthians 9:12; 11:9) occur, but the Greek word for **I fill up** without any compounds occurs only here in the Septuagint or New Testament. This Greek word signifies that the supply comes from an opposite quarter to the deficiency. The point of the apostle's boast is that Christ the sinless Master should have left something for Paul the unworthy servant to suffer. Similar in meaning, though not identical, is the expression in 2 Corinthians 1:5, where the sufferings of Christ are said to "flow over" the apostle.

What is still lacking. See 1 Corinthians 16:17; Philippians 2:30; 2 Corinthians 8:13-14; compare Luke 21:4.

In regard to Christ's afflictions. That is, which Christ endured. This seems to be the only natural interpretation of the words. Others have explained them as meaning "the afflictions imposed by Christ," or "the afflictions endured for Christ's sake," or "the afflictions which resemble those of Christ." All such interpretations put a more or less forced meaning on the genitive. All alike ignore the meaning of *anti* in the Greek word for **fill up**, *antanaplero*, which points to a distinction between the people suffering. Others again suppose the words to describe St. Paul's own afflictions regarded as Christ's because Christ suffers in his suffering church. Augustine follows this interpretation in his commentary on Psalm 142, where he also quotes Galatians 2:20. This last is a greatly favored explanation and has much to recommend it. But like the others it is open to the fatal objection that it empties the first preposition in *antanaplero* of any force. The central idea in this interpretation is the identification of the suffering apostle with the suffering Christ, whereas *antanaplero* emphasizes the distinction between the two. It is therefore inconsistent with this context, however important may be the truth which it expresses.

The theological difficulty which these and similar explanations are intended to remove is imaginary and not real. There is a sense in which it is quite legitimate to speak of Christ's afflictions as incomplete, a sense in which they may be, and indeed must be, supplemented, for the sufferings of Christ may be considered from two different points of view. They either have sacrificial efficacy or they have ministerial utility.

First, from the former point of view the passion of Christ was one full, perfect, and sufficient sacrifice, oblation, and satisfaction for the sins of the whole world. In this sense there could be nothing **lacking** in Christ's sufferings. Christ's sufferings are different in kind from those of his servants; the two are incommensurable. But in this sense the apostle would surely have used some other expression such as "the cross" (1:20; Ephesians 2:16) or "death" (1:22; Romans 5:10; Hebrews 2:14), but hardly **afflictions**. Indeed, "affliction" is not elsewhere applied in the New Testament in any sense to Christ's sufferings and certainly would not suggest a sacrificial act.

Second, from the latter point of view, it is a simple matter of fact that the afflictions of every saint and martyr do supplement the afflictions of Christ.

The church is built up by repeated acts of self-denial in successive individuals and successive generations. They continue the work which Christ began. They bear their part in the sufferings of Christ (2 Corinthians 1:7; Philippians 3:10); but St. Paul would have been the last to say that they bear their part in the atoning sacrifice of Christ. This being so, St. Paul does not mean to say that his own sufferings filled up all the "lack" but only went towards filling it up. These "lackings" will never be fully supplemented until the struggle of the church with sin and unbelief is brought to a close.

Thus the idea of expiation or satisfaction is wholly absent from this passage; and with it is removed the twofold temptation which has beset theologians of opposite schools. On the one hand Protestant commentators, rightly feeling that any interpretation which infringed the completeness of the work wrought by Christ's death must be wrong because it would make St. Paul contradict himself on a cardinal point of his teaching, have been tempted to wrest the sense of the words. They have emptied *antanaplero* of its proper force; or they have assigned a false meaning to **lacking**; or they have attached an unnatural sense to the genitive "of Christ" or **Christ's**.

On the other hand, Roman Catholic commentators, while protesting (as they had a right to do) against these methods of interpretation, have fallen into the opposite error. They have found in this passage an assertion of the merits of the saints and (as a necessary consequence) of the doctrine of indulgences. They have not observed that if the idea of vicarious satisfaction comes into the passage at all, the satisfaction of St. Paul is represented here as the same in kind with the satisfaction of Christ, however different it may be in degree. It is no part of a commentator here to inquire generally whether the Roman Catholic doctrine of the satisfaction of the saints can in any way be reconciled with St. Paul's doctrine of the satisfaction of Christ. It is sufficient to say that so far as this particular passage goes, the Roman Catholic doctrine can only be imported into it at the cost of a contradiction to the Pauline doctrine.

For the sake of his body. This antithetical form of expression obliges St. Paul to explain what he means by the body of Christ, **which is the church**; compare verse 18.

25. By the commission God . . . The word **commission** seems to have two senses: first, the actual administration of a household; second, the office of the administrator. For the former meaning see Ephesians 1:10; for the latter sense, which it has here, compare 1 Corinthians 9:17; Luke 16:2-4; Isaiah 22:19, 21. So the apostles and ministers of the church are called stewards, overseers (see 1 Corinthians 4:1-2; Titus 1:7: compare 1 Peter 4:10).

In its fullness. "To fulfill," that is, "to preach fully," "to give its complete development" (see Romans 15:19). Thus **the word of God** is here "the Gospel," as in most places (1 Corinthians 14:36; 2 Corinthians 2:17; 4:2), though not always (Romans 9:6), in other of St. Paul's letters and also in Acts.

26. The mystery. This is not the only term borrowed from the ancient mysteries which St. Paul employs to describe the teaching of the Gospel. The word **perfect** (verse 28) seems to be an extension of the same metaphor. In Philippians 4:12 we have, "I have learned the secret." But, whereas the heathen mysteries were strictly confined to a narrow circle, the Christian mysteries are freely communicated to all. There is therefore intentional paradox in the use of the image by St. Paul.

Thus the idea of secrecy or reserve disappears when **mystery** is adopted into the Christian vocabulary by St. Paul. The word signifies simply "a truth which was once hidden but now is revealed," "a truth which without special revelation would have been unknown." Of the nature of the truth itself the word says nothing. It may be transcendental, incomprehensible, mystical, mysterious, in the modern sense of the word (1 Corinthians 15:51; Ephesians 5:32); but this idea is quite accidental and must be gathered from the special circumstances of the case, for it cannot be inferred from the word itself. Hence **mystery** is almost universally found in connection with words denoting revelation or publication (see Romans 16:25-26; Ephesians 3:3, 5; 2 Thessalonians 2:7-8; 1 Timothy 3:16; 1 Corinthians 2:7; 14:2; 15:51).

But the one special **mystery** which absorbs St. Paul's thoughts in the letters to the Colossians and Ephesians is the free admission of the Gentiles on equal terms to the privileges of the covenant. For this he is a prisoner; this he is bound to proclaim fearlessly (4:3; Ephesians 6:19); this, though hidden from all time, was communicated to him by a special revelation (Ephesians 3:3); in this had God most signally displayed the lavish wealth of his goodness (Colossians 1:27; 2:2; Ephesians 1:9; 3:8-9). In one passage only throughout these two letters is **mystery** applied to anything else (Ephesians 5:32). The same idea of the **mystery** appears very prominently in the thanksgiving at the end of Romans (16:25).

27. Chosen. "Willed," "was pleased." It was God's grace; it came through no merit of their own.

Riches. The "wealth" of God as manifested in his dispensation of grace is a prominent idea in these letters; compare 2:2; Ephesians 1:7, 18; 3:8, 16.

Glorious. That is, "of the glorious manifestation." This word **glorious** in Hellenistic Greek is frequently used of a bright light (Luke 2:9; Acts 22:11; 1 Corinthians 15:41; 2 Corinthians 3:7). Hence it is applied generally to a divine disclosure, even where there is no physical accompaniment of light, and more especially to the revelation of God in Christ (John 1:14; 2 Corinthians 4:4).

Among the Gentiles. That is, "as exhibited among the Gentiles." It was just here that this **mystery**, this dispensation of grace, achieved its greatest triumphs and displayed its transcendent glory. Here too it was **riches**, for it overflowed all barriers of caste or race. Judaism was beggarly (Galatians 4:9) in comparison, since its treasures sufficed only for a few.

Christ in you. That is, "you Gentiles." Not Christ, but Christ given freely to the Gentiles, is the **mystery** of which St. Paul speaks.

28-29. We proclaim him, admonishing and teaching everyone with all wisdom, so that we may present everyone perfect in Christ. To this end I labor, struggling with all his energy, which so powerfully works in me.

This Christ we, the apostles and evangelists, proclaim without distinction and without reserve. We know no restriction either of people or of topics. We admonish every man and instruct every man. We initiate every man in all the mysteries of wisdom. It is our single aim to present every man fully and perfectly taught in Christ. For this end I train myself in the discipline of self-denial; for this end I commit myself to the arena of suffering and toil, putting forth in the conflict all that energy which he inspires, and which works in me so powerfully.

28. We. The preachers. The apostle hastens, as usual, to speak of the part which he was privileged to bear in this glorious dispensation. He is constrained to magnify his office.

Admonishing and teaching. These two words present complementary aspects of the preacher's duty. For the two functions of the preacher's office, corresponding respectively to these two words, see Paul's own language in Acts 20:20.

Everyone. This is repeated twice (in NIV; "every man" three times in KJV) for the sake of emphasizing the universality of the Gospel. This great truth, for which St. Paul gave his life, was now again endangered by the doctrine of an intellectual exclusiveness taught by the Gnosticizers at Colosse, as before it had been endangered by the doctrine of a ceremonial exclusiveness taught by the Judaizers in Galatia.

With all wisdom. The Gnostic spoke of a blind faith for the many, of a higher knowledge for the few. St. Paul declares that the fullest wisdom is offered to all alike. The character of the teaching is as free from restriction as are the qualifications of the recipients.

Perfect. See 1 Corinthians 2:6-7 (KJV). In both these passages the epithet **perfect** is probably a metaphor borrowed from the ancient mysteries, where it seems to have been applied to the fully instructed, as opposed to the novices. While using the favorite Gnostic term, the apostle strikes at the root of the Gnostic doctrine. The language descriptive of the heathen mysteries is transferred by him to the Christian dispensation, that he may thus more effectively contrast the things signified. The true Gospel also has its mysteries, its initiation; but these are open to all alike. In Christ every believer is **perfect**, for he has been admitted into its secrets.

29. To this end. That is, "that I may initiate all mankind in the fullness of this mystery," "that I may preach the Gospel to all without reserve." If

St. Paul had been content to preach an exclusive gospel, he might have saved himself from more than half the troubles of his life.

Labor. This word is used especially of the labor undergone by the athlete in his training and therefore fitly introduces the metaphor **struggling** (compare 1 Timothy 4:10).

> *2:1-3. I want you to know how much I am struggling for you and for those at Laodicea, and for all who have not met me personally. My purpose is that they may be encouraged in heart and united in love, so that they may have the full riches of complete understanding, in order that they may know the mystery of God, namely, Christ, in whom are hidden all the treasures of wisdom and knowledge.*

> *I spoke of an arena and a conflict in describing my apostolic labors. The image was not lightly chosen. I would have you know that my care is not confined to my own direct and personal disciples. I wish you to understand the magnitude of the struggle which my anxiety for you costs me—for you and for your neighbors of Laodicea, and for all who, like yourselves, have never met me face to face in the flesh. I am constantly wrestling in spirit, that the hearts of all such may be confirmed and strengthened in the faith; that they may be united in love; that they may attain to all the unspeakable wealth which comes from the firm conviction of an understanding mind, may be brought to the perfect knowledge of God's mystery, which is nothing else than Christ—Christ containing in himself all the treasures of wisdom and knowledge hidden away.*

1. Struggling. The area of the contest to which **struggling** in the preceding verse refers may be either outward or inward. It includes fightings without as well as fears within. Here, however, the inner struggle, the wrestling in prayer, is the predominant idea, as in 4:12.

Those at Laodicea. The Laodiceans were exposed to the same doctrinal perils as the Colossians. The Hierapolitans are doubtless included in **for all who have not met me personally** (compare 4:13) but are not mentioned here by name, probably because they were less closely connected with Colosse, and perhaps also because the danger was less threatening there.

For all who have not met me personally. "And all who, like yourselves, have not seen . . ." From a grammatical point of view, it is uncertain whether St. Paul's language here implies his personal acquaintance with his correspondents or the contrary. But in all such cases the sense of the context must be our guide. In the present instance **and for all** is quite out of place unless the Colossians and Laodiceans also were personally unknown to the apostle. There would be no meaning in singling out individuals who were known to him and then mentioning comprehensively all who were unknown to him. Hence we may infer from the expression here that St.

Paul had never visited Colosse. This accords with the incidental language of this letter elsewhere and with the direct historical narrative of the Acts.

2. Encouraged. "Confirmed," that is, "comforted" in the older and wider meaning of the word (*confortati*), but not with its modern and restricted sense (see Philippians 2:1).

In heart. They met the apostle heart to heart, though not face to face.

United. "They being united," for "united" must here have its common meaning, as it has elsewhere in this and in the companion letter (see verse 19 and Ephesians 4:16).

Mystery. The **mystery** here is not Christ, but "Christ as containing in himself all the full riches of complete understanding."

3. All. These repetitions serve to emphasize the character of the Gospel, which is as complete in itself as it is universal in its application.

Wisdom and knowledge. The two words occur together again in Romans 11:33 and 1 Corinthians 12:8. While **knowledge** is intuitive, **wisdom** is the process of reasoning also. While **knowledge** applies mainly to the understanding of truths, **wisdom** is additionally the power of reasoning about them and seeing what else they link up with.

Hidden. See 1 Corinthians 2:7. As before with "perfect" (1:28), here again in **hidden** (Greek *apokruphoi*) the apostle adapts a favorite term of the Gnostic teachers so that he may refute a favorite doctrine of theirs. The word *apocrypha* in the first instance was an honorable name given by the heretics themselves to their esoteric doctrines and their secret books. But owing to the general character of these works, the term, as adopted by orthodox writers, came to signify "false" and "spurious." The early fathers never applied it to the deutero-canonical writings but confined it to heretical works.

Colossians 2:4—3:4

Abide in the Truth of the Gospel (2:4-8)

4-8. I tell you this so that no one may deceive you by fine-sounding arguments. For though I am absent from you in body, I am present with you in spirit and delight to see how orderly you are and how firm your faith in Christ is. So then, just as you received Christ Jesus as Lord, continue to live in him, rooted and built up in him, strengthened in the faith as you were taught, and overflowing with thankfulness. See to it that no one takes you captive through hollow and deceptive philosophy, which depends on human tradition and the basic principles of this world rather than on Christ.

I do not say this without a purpose. I wish to warn you against anyone who wants to lead you astray by specious argument and persuasive rhetoric. For I am not an indifferent spectator of your doings. I am absent from you in my body, but I am present with you in my spirit. I rejoice to behold the orderly array and the solid phalanx which your faith toward Christ presents against the assaults of the foe. I entreat you therefore not to abandon the Christ, as you learnt from Epaphras to know him, even Jesus the Lord, but to continue to walk in him as you have done so far. I want you to be firmly rooted, once for all, in him. I desire to see you built up higher in him day by day, to see you growing even stronger and stronger through your faith, while you remain true to the lessons you have been taught, so that you may abound in it, and thus abounding may pour our your heart in gratitude to God, the giver of everything. Be on your guard; do not suffer yourselves to fall prey to certain people who would lead you captive by a hollow and deceitful system, which they call philosophy. They substitute the traditions of men for the truth of God. They enforce an elementary discipline of mundane ordinances fit only for children. Theirs is not the gospel of Christ.

4. I tell you this. "I say all this to you, lest you should be led astray by those false teachers who speak of another knowledge, of other mysteries."

The referent of **I tell you this** extends over verses 1-3 and involves two statements: first, the declaration that all knowledge is comprehended in Christ (verses 2-3); second, the expression of his own personal anxiety that they should remain steadfast in this conviction (verses 1-2). This last point explains the language which follows: **for though I am absent from you in body** (verse 5).

Deceive you. "Lead you astray by false reasoning." Compare James 1:22. It is not an uncommon word either in the Septuagint or in classical writers. The system against which St. Paul here contends professed to be a **philosophy** (verse 8) and had **an appearance of wisdom** (verse 23).

5. For. This frequently introduces the apodosis after "if" (Greek *ei*) in St. Paul (Romans 6:5-6; 1 Corinthians 9:2; 2 Corinthians 4:16-17; 13:4).

In spirit. "In my spirit," not "by the Spirit." We have here the common antithesis of flesh and spirit, or body and spirit; compare 1 Corinthians 5:3.

Delight to see. "Rejoicing and beholding." This must not be seen as a logical inversion. The contemplation of their orderly array, though it might have been first the cause, was afterwards the consequence of the apostle's rejoicing. He looked because it gave him satisfaction to look.

To see how orderly you are. "Your orderly array," a military metaphor. The enforced companionship of St. Paul with the soldiers of the praetorian guard at this time (Philippians 1:13) might have suggested this image. At all events, in the contemporary letter (see Ephesians 6:14ff.) we have an elaborate metaphor from a soldier's armor.

Firm. "Solid front, close phalanx," a continuation of the metaphor. Compare 1 Peter 5:9; Acts 16:5.

6. So then, just as you received Christ Jesus as Lord. That is, "Let your conviction and conduct be in perfect accordance with the doctrines and precepts of the Gospel as it was taught to you." For this use of **you received**—that is, "you received from your teachers, were instructed in"—compare 1 Corinthians 15:1, 3; Galatians 1:9; Philippians 4:9; 1 Thessalonians 2:13; 2 Thessalonians 3:6. The word **received** implies either "to receive as transmitted" or "to receive for transmission."

Christ. Christ rather than the Gospel because the central point in the Colossian heresy was the subversion of the true idea of the Christ.

Jesus as Lord, in whom the true conception of the Christ is realized; compare Ephesians 4:20-21, where the same idea is more directly expressed. The true teaching of Christ consists of, first, the recognition of the historical person Jesus, and, second, the acceptance of him as the Lord.

This teaching was put at serious risk by the mystic theosophy of the false teachers.

7. Built up in him. "Being built up," as in 1 Corinthians 3:10-14. **In him** because in this letter Christ is represented as the binding element rather than as the foundation of the building. The repetition of **in him** emphasizes the main idea of the passage, and indeed of the whole letter.

In the faith. Faith is, as it were, the cement of the building.

As you were taught. That is, "remaining true to the lessons which you received from Epaphras, and not being led astray by any later pretenders"; compare 1:6-7.

Overflowing with thankfulness. The same ending occurs in 4:2. Thanksgiving is the intended end of all human conduct, whether exhibited in words or in deeds.

8. Takes you captive. "Makes you his prey, carries you off body and soul." The Colossians had been rescued from the bondage of darkness, they had been transferred to the kingdom of light, they had been settled there as free citizens (1:12-13); but now there was danger that they should fall into a state worse than their former slavery, that they should be carried off as so much booty. Compare 2 Timothy 3:6.

Through hollow and deceptive philosophy. "Through philosophy which is empty and deceptive." It should be remembered that in this later age, owing to Roman influence, the term **philosophy** was used to describe practical as well as speculative systems; so it covered the ascetic life as well as the mystic theosophy of these Colossian heretics. Hence the apostle is here flinging back at these false teachers a favorite term of their own, "their vaunted philosophy, which is hollow and misleading."

The word indeed could claim a truly noble origin, for it is said to have arisen out of the humility of Pythagoras, who called himself "a lover of wisdom." In such a sense the term would entirely accord with the spirit and teaching of St. Paul, for it bore testimony to the insufficiency of the human intellect and the need of a revelation. But in his age it had come to be associated with the idea of subtle dialectics and profitless speculation. In this particular instance it was combined with a mystic cosmogony and angelology which contributed a fresh element of danger.

As contrasted with the power and fullness and certainty of revelation, all such philosophy was "foolish" (1 Corinthians 1:20). It is worth observing that this word, which to the Greeks denoted the highest effort of the intellect, occurs only here in St. Paul's writings, just as he uses "admirable," which was their term to express the highest moral excellence, in a single passage only (Philippians 4:8). The reason is much the same in both cases. The Gospel had deposed the terms inadequate to the highest standard, whether of knowledge or of practice, which it had introduced.

Through . . . The false teaching is described, first, in terms of its source—human tradition, and, second, in terms of its content—**principles of this world.**

Tradition. Other systems, like the ceremonial *Mishnah* of the Pharisees, might correctly be described in this way (Matthew 15:2ff.; Mark 7:3ff.); but this description was peculiarly appropriate to a mystic theosophy like this of the Colossian false teachers. The teaching might be oral or written, but it was essentially esoteric, essentially traditional. It could not appeal to sacred books which were in front of the world for centuries.

The basic principles. "The rudiments, the elementary teaching"; compare verse 20. The same phrase occurs again in Galatians 4:3. As **basic principles** signifies primarily "the letters of the alphabet," so as a secondary meaning it denotes "rudimentary instruction."

Of this world. That is, "belonging to the sphere of material and external things."

On Christ. The apostle seems to say, "You have attained the liberty and the intelligence of manhood; do not submit yourselves again to a rudimentary discipline fit only for children. In Christ you have been exalted into the sphere of the Spirit; do not plunge yourselves again into the atmosphere of material and sensuous things."

The Truth Stated Positively and Negatively (2:9-15)

9-15. For in Christ all the fullness of the Deity lives in bodily form, and you have been given fullness in Christ, who is the head over every power and authority. In him you were also circumcised, in the putting off of the sinful nature, not with a circumcision done by the hands of men but with the circumcision done by Christ, having been buried with him in baptism and raised with him through your faith in the power of God, who raised him from the dead. When you were dead in your sins and in the uncircumcision of your sinful nature, God made you alive with Christ. He forgave us all our sins, having canceled the written code, with its regulations, that was against us and that stood opposed to us; he took it away, nailing it to the cross. And having disarmed the powers and authorities, he made a public spectacle of them, triumphing over them by the cross.

In Christ the entire fullness of the Godhead abides forever, having united itself with man by taking a human body. And so in him—not in any inferior mediators—you have your life, your being, for you are filled from his fullness. He, I say, is the head over all spiritual beings—call them principalities or powers or what you will. In him too you have the true circumcision—the circumcision which is not made with hands but wrought by the Spirit—the circumcision which divests not of a part only but of the whole carnal body—the circumcision which is not of Moses but of Christ. This circumcision you have because you were buried with Christ to your old selves beneath the baptismal waters and were raised with him from those same waters to a new and regenerate life through your faith in the powerful working of God who raised him from the dead. Yes, you—you Gentiles who before were dead, when you walked in your transgressions and in the uncircumcision of your unchastened carnal heathen heart—even you did God bring alive together with Christ, then and there freely forgiving all of us—Jews and Gentiles alike—all our transgressions, then and there canceling the bond which stood valid against us (for it bore our own signature), the bond which engaged us to fulfill all the law of ordinances, which was our stern pitiless tyrant. Yes, this very bond Christ has put out of sight forever, nailing it to his cross and rending it with his body and killing it in his death. Taking on him our human nature, he stripped off and cast aside all the powers of evil which clung to it like a poisonous garment. As a mighty conqueror he displayed these his fallen enemies to an astonished world, leading them in triumph on his cross.

9-15. In explaining the true teaching according to Christ, St. Paul condemns the two false principles which lay at the root of this heretical teaching: first, the theological error of substituting inferior and created beings, angelic mediators, for the divine Head himself (verses 9-10), and, second, the practical error of insisting on ritual and ascetic observances as the foundation of their moral teaching (verses 11-15). Their theological speculations and their ethical code alike were at fault.

9. For in Christ . . . The apostle justifies the foregoing charge that this doctrine was not according to Christ. "In Christ dwells the whole *pleroma*, the entire fullness of the Godhead, whereas they represent it to you as dispersed among several spiritual agencies. Christ is the one fountainhead of all spiritual life, whereas they teach you to seek it in communion with inferior creatures." The same truths have been stated before (1:14ff.) more generally, and they are now restated, with direct and immediate reference to the heretical teaching.

All the fullness. "The totality of the divine powers and attributes."

In bodily form. "Bodily-wise," "corporeally," that is, "assuming a bodily form, becoming incarnate." This is in addition to the previous statement in 1:19, **For God was pleased to have all his fullness dwell in him.** The indwelling of the *pleroma*, **fullness,** refers to the eternal Word. But **bodily** is added to show that the Word, in whom the *pleroma* thus had its abode from all eternity, crowned his work by the Incarnation. Thus while St. Paul's main statement **in Christ all the fullness of the Deity lives in bodily form** corresponds to the opening sentence of St. John, "In the beginning was the Word, and the Word was with God, and the Word was God," the subsidiary adverb **bodily** of St. Paul has its counterpart in the additional statement of St. John, "The Word became flesh" (John 1:14). All other meanings which have been assigned to **bodily** here, such as "wholly" or "really" or "essentially," are unsupported by usage. Nor again can the body be thought of as anything but Christ's human body, as part of the created world.

10. In Christ. True life consists in union with him, and not in dependence on any inferior being.

You have been given fullness. "Your fullness comes from his fullness; his *pleroma* is transfused into you by virtue of your incorporation in him." See John 1:16; Ephesians 3:19; 4:13. Hence also the church, as ideally regarded, is called the **fullness** of Christ because all his graces and energies are communicated to her; see Ephesians 1:23.

The head. This image expresses much more than the idea of sovereignty; the head is also the center of vital force, the source of all energy and life.

Over every power and authority. And therefore over those angelic beings whom the false teachers adopted as mediators, thus transferring to the inferior members the allegiance due to the Head; compare verse 19.

11. The previous verses have dealt with the theological tenets of the false teachers. The apostle now turns to their practical errors: "You do not need the circumcision of the flesh; for you have received the circumcision of the heart. There are three distinguishing features of this higher circumcision. First, it is not external but internal, not made with hands but by the Spirit. Second, it divests not of a part only of the flesh, but of the whole body of evil human desires. Third, it is the circumcision not of Moses or of the patriarchs but of Christ." Thus it is distinguished as regards, first, its character, second, its extent, and third, its author.

Circumcised. The moment at which this is conceived as taking place is defined by the other aorists, **buried** and **raised** (verse 12), as the time of their baptism, when they "put on Christ."

Not ... done by the hands of men. That is, "immaterial," "spiritual," as in Mark 14:58 and 2 Corinthians 5:1.

Done by ... done by. These words were chosen to express the completeness of the spiritual change. It is not a part of the body but the whole body which is thus cast aside. Thus the idea of completeness is brought out both in the energy of the action and in the extent of its operation; compare 3:9, which underlines this idea of completeness with the total discarding of the **old self.**

Putting off of the sinful nature (NIV margin: **flesh**) "The whole body which consists of the flesh," that is, "the body with all its corrupt and carnal affections," as in 3:5. See also Romans 6:6; 7:24; Philippians 3:21.

12. Baptism is the grave of the old man and the birth of the new. As he sinks beneath the baptismal waters, the believer buries there all his corrupt affections and past sins; as he emerges from there, he rises regenerate, quickened to new hopes and a new life. This it is because it is not only the crowning act of his own faith but also the seal of God's adoption and the earnest of God's Spirit. Thus baptism is an image of his participation both in the death and in the resurrection of Christ. For this twofold image, as it presents itself to St. Paul, see especially Romans 6:3ff.

In baptism. "In the act of baptism." A distinction seems to be observed elsewhere in the New Testament between baptism correctly called by this name and "washing" of different kinds, of "cups, pitchers and kettles" in Mark 7:4 and "ceremonial washings" in Hebrews 9:10. Doubtless physical baptism was more appropriate to describe the one final and complete act of Christian baptism.

Through your faith in the power of God, who raised him from the dead. Only by a belief in the resurrection are the benefits of the resurrection obtained, because only so are its moral effects produced. Hence St. Paul prays that he may "know . . . the power of his resurrection" (Philippians 3:10). Hence too he makes the cardinal article in the Christian's creed, "If you . . . believe in your heart that God raised him from the dead, you will be saved" (Romans 10:9).

13. When you. That is, "you Gentiles."

Dead in your sins. "Sins" are the actual definite transgressions, while **the uncircumcision of your sinful nature** is the impure cardinal disposition which prompts them.

The uncircumcision of your sinful nature. The external fact is here mentioned not for its own sake but for its symbolical meaning. The outward uncircumcision of the Gentiles is a type of their unchastened carnal mind. In other words, though the literal meaning is not excluded, the spiritual reference is most prominent, as appears from verse 11.

Made you alive. It has been questioned whether the life here spoken of should be understood in a spiritual sense as the regeneration of the moral being or in the literal sense as the future life of immortality regarded as conferred on the Christian potentially now, though only to be realized hereafter. But is not such an issue altogether superfluous? Is there any reason to think that Paul would have separated these two ideas of life? To him the future glorified life is only the continuation of the present moral and spiritual life. The two are the same in essence, however the details may differ. Moral and spiritual regeneration is salvation and life.

He forgave us. "Having forgiven," as in Luke 7:41ff.; 2 Corinthians 2:7, 10; 12:13; Ephesians 4:32. The idea of sin as a debt incurred to God (Matthew 6:12) underlies this expression. The image is carried out in the canceled written code (Colossians 2:14).

Us. The person is changed; "not to you Gentiles only, but to us all alike." St. Paul is eager to claim his share in the transgression, that he may claim it also in the forgiveness. For other examples of the change from the second to the first person, see 1:10-13; 3:3-4 (NIV margin); Ephesians 2:2-3, 13-14; 5:2. See also Galatians 3:25-26; 4:5-6, where there is the converse transition.

14. Having canceled the written code. "The bond standing against us." The word translated "written code," which means an autograph of any kind, is used almost exclusively for a handwritten note, a bond or obligation having the "sign-manual" of the debtor or contractor.

In this verse the Jewish people might be said to have signed the contract when they bound themselves by a curse to observe all the enactments of the law (Deuteronomy 27:14-26); and the primary reference would be to them. But **against us** and **to us** seem to include Gentiles as well as Jews; so a wider reference must be given to the expression. The **regulations** therefore, though referring primarily to the Mosaic ordinances, will include all forms of positive decrees in which moral and social principles are embodied or religious duties defined; and "the written code" is the moral assent of the conscience which (as it were) signs and seals the obligation. The Gentiles, though they "do not have the law . . . are a law for themselves" (Romans 2:14-15).

With its regulations. "Consisting in ordinances"; compare Ephesians 2:15. The word "regulations" is used here in its proper sense of a "decree," "ordinance," corresponding to "rules" (see verse 20). This is its only sense in the New Testament (see Luke 2:1 and Acts 17:7—the emperor's decrees; Acts 16:4—the apostolic ordinances).

Nailing it to the cross. "The abrogation was even more emphatic. Not only was the writing erased, but the document itself was torn up and thrown aside." By **nailing** is meant that the law of ordinances was nailed to the cross, torn with Christ's body, and destroyed with his death. It has been supposed that in some cities the abrogation of a decree was signified by running a nail through it and hanging it up in public. The image would thus gain force, but there is no distinct evidence of such a custom.

15. Disarmed. This word appears not to occur at all before St. Paul and rarely, if ever, after his time. The occurrence of this word here and in 3:9 and 2:11 (**putting off**) is remarkable. The choice of an unusual, if not a wholly new word must have been prompted by the desire to emphasize the completeness of the action. The Greek fathers translated this verse, "having stripped off and put away the powers of evil," making "disarmed" govern "the powers and authorities." (See Chrysostom, Severianus, Theodore of Mopsuestia, and Theodoret.)

The meaning then will be as follows: Christ took upon himself our human nature with all its temptations (Hebrews 4:15). The powers of evil gathered about him. Again and again they assailed him; but each fresh assault ended in a new defeat. In the wilderness he was tempted by Satan;

but Satan retired for the time, baffled and defeated (Luke 4:13). Through the voice of his chief disciple the temptation was renewed, and he was entreated to decline his appointed sufferings and death. Satan was again driven off (Matthew 16:23). Then the last hour came. This was the great crisis of all, when "darkness" reigned (Luke 22:53), when the prince of this world asserted his tyranny (John 12:31). The final act in the conflict began with the agony in Gethsemane; it ended with the cross of Calvary. The victory was complete. The enemy of mankind was defeated. The powers of evil, which had clung like a Nessus robe about his humanity, were torn off and thrown aside forever. And the victory of mankind is involved in the victory of Christ. In his cross we too are divested of the poisonous, clinging garments of temptation and sin and death. For the image of the garments compare Isaiah 64:6, but especially Zechariah 3:1ff. In this prophetic passage the image is used of the prophet's type and namesake, the Jesus of the Restoration, not in his own person, but as the high priest and representative of a guilty but cleansed and forgiven people, with whom he is identified.

The above interpretation is grammatical; it accords with St. Paul's teaching, and it is commended by the parallel uses of the substantive in verse 11. The "disarming" accomplished in us when we are baptized into his death is a counterpart to the "disarming" which he accomplished by his death. With him indeed it was only the temptation; with us it is the sin as well as the temptation. But otherwise the parallel is complete. In both cases it is a putting off of the powers of evil, a liberation from the dominion of sinful nature.

The powers and authorities. What **powers** are especially meant here will appear from Ephesians 6:12.

A public spectacle. "Displayed" as a victor displays his captives or trophies in a triumphal procession. Nowhere does this word convey the idea of "making an example" but signifies simply "to display, publish, proclaim."

Public. "Boldly," not "publicly." The idea of publicity may sometimes be connected with the word as a secondary idea, e.g. in John 7:4, but it does not displace the primary sense.

Triumphing over them. "Leading them in triumph," the same metaphor as in 2 Corinthians 2:14, where it is wrongly translated in the KJV "causeth us to triumph." Here, however, the defeated powers of evil are in view; there the people who have submitted to Christ are led in public, chained to Christ's triumphal carriage. This is the correct meaning of "triumph" as found elsewhere.

By the cross (NIV margin, **in them** or **in him**). The paradox of the crucifixion is placed in the strongest light—triumph in helplessness and glory in shame. The convict's gibbet is the victor's carriage.

Obligations Which Follow (2:16—3:4)

16-19. Therefore do not let anyone judge you by what you eat or drink, or with regard to a religious festival, a New Moon celebration or a Sabbath day. These are a shadow of the things that were to come; the reality, however, is found in Christ. Do not let anyone who delights in false humility and the worship of angels disqualify you for the prize. Such a person goes into great detail about what he has seen, and his unspiritual mind puffs him up with idle notions. He has lost connection with the Head, from whom the whole body, supported and held together by its ligaments and sinews, grows as God causes it to grow.

Seeing then that the bond is canceled, that the law of ordinances is repealed, beware of subjecting yourselves to its tyranny again. Suffer no man to call you to account in the matter of eating or drinking, or again over the observance of a festival or a new moon or a sabbath. These are only shadows thrown in advance, only types of things to come. The substance, the reality, in every case belongs to the Gospel of Christ. The prize is now fairly within your reach. Do not suffer yourselves to be robbed of it by any stratagem of the false teachers. Their religion is an officious humility which displays itself in the worship of angels. They make a parade of their visions, but they are following an empty phantom. They profess humility, but they are puffed up with their vaunted wisdom, which is after all only the mind of the flesh. Meanwhile, they have substituted inferior spiritual agencies for the One true Mediator, the Eternal Word. Clinging to these lower intelligences, they have lost their hold on the Head; they have severed their link with him on whom the whole body depends, from whom it derives its vitality, and to whom it owes its unity, being supplied with nourishment and knit together in one by means of the several joints and attachments, so that it grows with a growth which comes from God himself.

16ff. The two main tendencies of the Colossian heresy are discernible in this warning (verses 16-19), as they were in the previous statement (verses 9-15). Here, however, the order is reversed. The practical error, an excessive ritualism and ascetic rigor, is first dealt with (verses 16-17); the theological error, the interposition of angelic mediators, follows (verses 18-19). The first is the substitution of a shadow for the substance; the second is the preference of an inferior member to the Head. The reversal of order is due to the link between the paragraphs, the opening subject in the second paragraph being a continuation of the concluding subject in the first, by the figure called chiasm; compare Galatians 4:5.

16. Judge you. Not "condemn you," but "take you to task," as in Romans 14:3ff. The judgment may or may not end in an acquittal, but in any case it is wrong, since these matters ought not to be taken as the basis of a judgment.

By what you eat or drink. See Romans 14:17; Hebrews 9:10; 1 Corinthians 8:8. The first indication that the Mosaic distinctions of things clean and unclean should be abolished was given by our Lord himself (Mark 7:14ff.). They were later formally annulled by the vision which St. Peter had (Acts 10:11ff.). The ordinances of the Mosaic law applied almost exclusively to meats. It contained no prohibitions about drinks except in a few cases—e.g., priests ministering in the tabernacle (Leviticus 10:9), liquids contained in unclean vessels, etc. (Leviticus 11:34, 36), and Nazirite vows (Numbers 6:3).

The rigor of the Colossian false teachers, however, like that of their Jewish prototypes, the Essenes, doubtless went far beyond the injunctions of the law. It is probable that they forbade wine and animal food altogether. For allusions in St. Paul to similar observances not required by the law, see Romans 14:2, 21; 1 Timothy 4:2-3.

A religious festival, a New Moon celebration or a Sabbath day. The same three words occur together as an exhaustive enumeration of the sacred times among the Jews in 1 Chronicles 23:31, 2 Chronicles 2:4, 31:3, Ezekiel 45:17, and Hosea 2:11. See also Galatians 4:10, where the first three words correspond to the three words used here, though the order is reversed.

A Sabbath day. "A Sabbath day," not, as in the KJV, "sabbath days." The observance of sacred times was an integral part of the old dispensation. Under the new they have ceased to have any value except as a means to an end. The great principle that "the Sabbath was made for man and not man for the Sabbath," though underlying the Mosaic ordinances, was first distinctly pronounced by our Lord. The setting apart of special days for God's service is a confession of our imperfect state, an admission that we cannot or do not devote our whole time to him. Sabbaths will ultimately be superseded when our life becomes one eternal sabbath. Meanwhile, the apostle's rebuke warns us against attributing to any holy days whatever a meaning and an importance which is alien to the spirit of the new covenant.

17. Two ideas are prominent in this image. First, the contrast between the ordinances of the law and the teaching of the Gospel, as the shadow and the substance respectively; second, the conception of the shadow as thrown before the substance. Thus it implies both the unsubstantiality and the supercession of the Mosaic ritual.

The reality, however, is found in Christ. As the shadow belonged to Moses, so the substance belongs to Christ; that is, the reality, the antitype, in each case is found in the Christian dispensation. Thus the Passover typifies the atoning sacrifice, the unleavened bread—the purity and sincerity of the true believer, the Pentecostal feast—the ingathering of the first fruits, the Sabbath—the rest of God's people.

18. The Christian's career is the contest of the stadium (Acts 20:24; 2 Timothy 4:7); Christ is the umpire, the dispenser of the rewards (2 Timothy 4:8); eternal life is the wreath, the victor's prize (1 Corinthians 9:24; Philippians 3:14). The Colossians were in a good position to win this prize. They had entered the competitions, and they were running well; but the false teachers, thrusting themselves in the way, attempted to trip them up or otherwise impede them in the race and thus rob them of their just reward.

Disqualify you for the prize. "Rob you of the prize." The false teachers at Colosse are not regarded as umpires nor as successful rivals but simply as people frustrating those who otherwise would have won the prize. The word **disqualify** is broad enough to include such meanings.

Humility. Humility is a vice with heathen moralists but a virtue with Christian apostles. In this passage, which (with verse 23) forms the sole exception to the general language of the apostles, the divergence is rather apparent than real. The disparagement is in the accompaniments and not in the word itself. Humility, when it becomes self-conscious, ceases to have any value; and self-consciousness at least, if not affection, is implied by **delights in.** Moreover, the character of the **humility** in this case is further defined as **worship of angels**, which was altogether a perversion of the truth.

Worship. There was an official parade of humility in selecting these lower beings as intercessors rather than appealing directly to the throne of grace. The word refers to the external rites of religion and signifies an over-scrupulous devotion to external forms.

Puffs him up. Their profession of humility was a cloak for excessive pride (see 1 Corinthians 8:1).

With idle notions. "The mind of the flesh" (cf. KJV), that is, unenlightened by the Spirit (compare Romans 8:7). It would seem that the apostle is here taking up some watchword of the false teachers. They doubtless boasted that they were directed "by the mind." Yes, he answers, but it is "the mind of the flesh."

19. The Head. The supplication and worship of angels is a substitution of inferior members for the Head, who is the only source of spiritual life and energy.

Ligaments. The Greek word for **ligaments**, like the English word, has a general and a special sense. In its general and comprehensive meaning it denotes any of the connecting sinews which hold the body together, such as muscles or tendons or ligaments; in its special and restricted use it is a technical term.

The two functions performed by the **ligaments** and **sinews** are, first, the supply of nutrients, etc. (**supported**) and, second, the compacting of the frame (**held together**). In other words, they perform the communication of life and energy and the preservation of unity and order. The source (**from whom**) is Christ himself, the **Head**; but the channels of communication are the different members of his body in relation to one another.

In the parallel passage, Ephesians 4:16, this part of the image is more distinctly emphasized, "joined and held together by every supporting ligament." The difference reflects the different aims of the two letters. In the Colossian letter the vital link with the Head is the main theme, in the Ephesian the unity in diversity among the members.

Grows as God causes it to grow. By the twofold means of contact and attachment, nutriment has been diffused, and structural unity has been attained. But these are not the ultimate result; they are only intermediate processes. The end is growth.

As God. That is, "which partakes of God, which belongs to God, which has its abode in God." Thus the finite is truly united with the Infinite; the end which the false teachers strove in vain to accomplish is attained. The Gospel vindicates itself as the true theanthropism (the doctrine of the union of the divine and human natures), after which the human heart is yearning and the human intellect is feeling.

Concerning the conclusion of the sentence, contrast the parallel passage in Ephesians 4:16, where again the different endings are determined by the different motives of the two letters.

The discoveries of modern physiology have invested the apostle's language with far greater distinctness and force than it would have had with his contemporaries. Any exposition of the nervous system reads like a commentary on the image of the relationship between the body and the head. At every turn we meet with some fresh illustration which kindles it with a flood of light. The volition communicated from the brain to the limbs, the sensations of the extremities telegraphed back to the brain, the absolute mutual sympathy between the head and the members, the instantaneous paralysis if the supply line is cut—all these add to the completeness and life of the image. We cannot fail to be struck in the text not only with the correctness of Paul's imagery but also with the propriety of the terms; and we are forcibly reminded that among the apostle's most intimate companions at this time was one whom he calls "our dear friend Luke, the doctor" (4:14).

20-23. Since you died with Christ to the basic principles of this world, why, as though you still belonged to it, do you submit to its rules: "Do not handle! Do not taste! Do not touch!"? These are all destined to perish with use, because they are based on human commands and teachings. Such regulations indeed have an appearance of wisdom, with their self-

imposed worship, their false humility and their harsh treatment of the body, but they lack any value in restraining sensual indulgence.

You died with Christ to your old life. All mundane relations have ceased for you. Why then do you—you who have attained your spiritual manhood—submit still to the rudimentary discipline of children? Why do you—you who are citizens of heaven—bow your necks afresh to the tyranny of material ordinances as though you were still living in the world? It is the same old story again; the same round of hard, meaningless, vexatious prohibitions, "Handle not," "Taste not," "Touch not." What folly! All these things—these meats and drinks and the like—are earthly, perishable, wholly trivial and unimportant! They have already been used, and there is an end of them. What is this but to draw down on yourselves the denunciations uttered by the prophet of old? What is this but to abandon God's word for precepts which are issued by human authority and inculcated by human teachers? All such things have a show of wisdom, I grant. There is an officious parade of religious devotion, an eager affectation of humility; there is a stern ascetic rigor which ill-treats the body. But there is nothing of any real value to check indulgence of the flesh.

20. From the theological tenets of the false teachers the apostle turns to the ethical—from the objects of their worship to the principles of their conduct. The baptism of Christ, he argues, is death to the world. The Christian has passed into another sphere of existence. Mundane ordinances have ceased to have any value for him because his mundane life has ended. They belong to the category of the perishable; he has been translated to the region of the eternal. It is therefore a denial of his Christianity to subject himself again to their tyranny, to return once more to the dominion of the world.

Since you died. For this link between baptism and death see 2:12 and 3:3. This death has many aspects in Paul's teaching. It is not only a dying with Christ (2 Timothy 2:11), but it is also a dying to or from something. This is sometimes represented as sin (Romans 6:2), sometimes as self (2 Corinthians 5:14-15), sometimes as the law (Romans 7:6; Galatians 2:19). In every case Paul uses the aorist tense of "died," for he wants to emphasize the one absolute crisis which was marked by the change of changes.

To the basic principles of this world. That is, "from the rudimentary, disciplinary ordinances whose sphere is the mundane and sensuous."

21. **"Do not handle! ..."** The apostle disparagingly repeats the prohibitions of the false teachers in their own words, **"Do not handle! Do not taste! Do not touch!"**

These prohibitions relate to defilement contracted in different ways by contact with impure objects. Some were doubtless reenactments of the

Mosaic law, while others would be exaggerations or additions of a rigorous asceticism such as we find among the Essene prototype of these Colossian heretics—for example, the avoidance of oil, wine, or meat, the shunning of contact with a stranger or a religious inferior, and the like.

22. Only consider what is the real import of this scrupulous avoidance. Why are you attributing an inherent value to things which are fleeting? You yourselves are citizens of eternity, and yet your thoughts are absorbed in the perishable.

To perish with use. "In the consuming." The unusual word here was chosen for its expressiveness. The things could not be used without making them unfit for further use. The subtlety of the expression in the original cannot be reproduced by any translation.

They are based on human commands and teachings. The coincidences in St. Paul's language here with our Lord's words in Matthew 15:1-20 and Mark 7:1-23 are striking and suggest that the apostle had this discourse in his mind. First, both argue against these vexatious ordinances from the standpoint of the perishableness of meats. Second, both insist on the indifference of such things in themselves. In Mark 7:19 the evangelist emphasizes the importance of our Lord's words on this occasion as practically abolishing the Mosaic distinction of meats by declaring all foods alike to be clean. Third, both link such ordinances with the practices condemned in the prophetic denunciation of Isaiah.

23. All such teaching is worthless. It may bear the semblance of wisdom, but it lacks the reality. It may make an officious parade of religious service; it may vaunt its humility; it may treat the body with merciless rigor. But it entirely fails in its chief aim. It is powerless to check indulgence of the flesh.

Self-imposed worship. "In volunteered, self-imposed, officious, supererogatory service." One or both of these two ideas—first, "excessive readiness, officious zeal"; second, "affectation, unreality"—are involved in this and similar compounds.

St. Paul apparently has in front of him some exposition of the views of the Colossian heretics, either in writing or (more probably) from a report from Epaphras. In reply he altogether denies the claims of this system to the title of **wisdom**; he disputes the value of these **human commands** (verse 22); he allows that this **sensual indulgence** is the great evil to be checked, the fatal disease to be cured. But he will not agree that the remedies prescribed have any substantial and lasting efficacy.

3:1-4. Since then, you have been raised with Christ, set your hearts on things above, where Christ is seated at the right hand of God. Set your minds on things above, not on earthly things. For you died, and your life is now hidden with Christ in God. When Christ, who is your life, appears, then you also will appear with him in glory.

If this be so, if you were raised with Christ, if you were translated into heaven, what follows? Why, you must realize the change. All your aims must center in heaven, where reigns the Christ who has thus exalted you, enthroned on God's right hand. All your thoughts must abide in heaven, not on the earth. For, I say it once again, you have nothing to do with mundane things: you died once for all to the world: you are living another life. This life indeed is hidden now: it has no outward splendor as men count splendor; for it is a life with Christ, a life in God. But the veil will not always shroud it. Christ, our life, will be manifested hereafter; then you also will be manifested with him and the world will see your glory.

1. Since, then, you have been raised with Christ. The sacrament of baptism, as administered in the apostolic age, involved a twofold symbolism: a death or burial and a resurrection. In the rite itself these were represented by two distinct acts, the disappearance beneath the water and the emergence from the water. But in the change typified by the rite, they are two aspects of the same thing, "like the concave and convex in a circle," to use an old simile. The negative side—the death and burial—implies the positive side—the resurrection.

The change involved in baptism, if truly realized, must pervade a man's whole nature. It affects not only his practical conduct but his intellectual conceptions also. It is nothing less than a removal into a new sphere of being. He is translated from earth to heaven; and with this translation his point of view is altered, his standard of judgment is wholly changed. Matter is to him no longer the great enemy; his position toward it is one of absolute neutrality. Ascetic rules, ritual ordinances, have ceased to have any absolute value, irrespective of their effects. All these things are of the earth, earthly. The material, the transitory, the mundane, has given place to the moral, the eternal, the heavenly.

Set your hearts on things above. Cease to concentrate your energies, your thoughts, on mundane ordinances, and realize your new and heavenly life, of which Christ is the polestar.

Where Christ is seated at the right hand of God. Christ's being seated implies that the believer is also seated. See Ephesians 2:4-6; compare Revelation 3:21.

2. Things above. The same expression is repeated for emphasis. "You must not only *seek* heaven; you must also *think* heaven."

3. For you died. In baptism. The aorist **died** denotes the past act, the perfect **hidden** the permanent effects.

Hidden. "Buried out of sight." The apostle's argument is this: "When you sank under the baptismal water, you disappeared forever to the world. You rose again, it is true, but you rose only to God. The world from then on knows nothing of your new life, and (as a consequence) your new life must know nothing of the world."

4. Christ. A fourth occurrence of the name of Christ in this context; compare verse 1, "with Christ" and "where Christ," verse 3 "with Christ." A pronoun would have been more natural but less emphatic.

Your life (some manuscripts **our**). This is an advance on the previous statement, **your life is now hidden with Christ** (verse 3), in two respects. First, it is not enough to have said that life is shared **with** Christ. The apostle declares that life **is** Christ. Compare 1 John 5:12. Second, **your** replaces **our** (KJV). The apostle hastens to include himself among the recipients of the bounty.

Then you also will appear with him. The veil which now shrouds your higher life from others, and even partly from yourselves, will then be withdrawn. The world which persecutes, despises, ignores now will then be blinded with the dazzling glory of the revelation. Compare 1 John 3:1-2.

In glory. See John 17:22; Romans 8:17.

Colossians 3:5—4:6

Comprehensive Rules (3:5-17)

*5-11. Put to death, therefore, whatever belongs to your earthly nature:
sexual immorality, impurity, lust, evil desires and greed, which is idolatry. Because of these, the wrath of God is coming. You used to walk in
these ways, in the life you once lived. But now you must rid yourselves of
all such things as these: anger, rage, malice, slander, and filthy language
from your lips. Do not lie to each other, since you have taken off your old
self with its practices and have put on the new self, which is being
renewed in knowledge in the image of its Creator. Here there is no Greek
or Jew, circumcised or uncircumcised, barbarian, Scythian, slave or free,
but Christ is all, and is in all.*

*So then realize this death to the world; kill all your earthly members. Is it
fornication, impurity of whatever kind, passion, evil desire? Or again, is it
that covetousness which makes a religion, an idolatry of greed? Do not
deceive yourselves. For all these things God's wrath will surely come. In
these sins you, like other Gentiles, indulged in times past, when your life was
spent among them. But now everything is changed. Now you also must put
away not this or that desire, but all sins, whatever they are. Anger, wrath,
malice, slander, filthy abuse; banish it from your lips. Be not false to each
other in word or deed; but throw off forever the old man with his actions,
and put on the new, who is renewed from day to day, growing to perfect
knowledge and refashioned after the image of his Creator. In this new life,
in this regenerate man, there is not, there cannot be, any distinction between
Greek or Jew, between circumcision or uncircumcision; there is no room for
barbarian, for Scythian, for slave or free. Christ has displaced, has annihilated, all these; Christ is himself all things and in all things.*

5. The false teachings of the Gnostics had failed to check **sensual indulgence** (2:23). The true teaching of the apostle has power to kill the whole carnal man. The substitution of a comprehensive principle for special precepts—of the heavenly life in Christ for a code of minute ordinances—eventually achieves the goal which the Gnostic teachers have striven, and striven in vain, to reach.

Put to death. "Carry out this principle of death to the world (2:20; 3:3), and kill everything that is mundane and carnal in your being."

Whatever belongs to your earthly nature. Each person has a twofold moral personality. There is in him the **old man**, and there is in him also **the new man** (verses 9-10, KJV). The old man with all his members must be pitilessly slain. It is plain that **earthly nature** here is used, like **self** in verse 9, not physically, but morally. For this use of the physical as a symbol of the moral, of which it is the potential instrument, compare Matthew 5:29ff.

Sexual immorality, impurity . . . The general order is from the less comprehensive to the more comprehensive. Thus **sexual immorality** is a special kind of uncleanness, while **lust** is uncleanness in any form; see Ephesians 5:3; compare Galatians 5:19. Again, **evil desires**, though frequently referring to this class of sins (Romans 1:26), would include other base passions which do not fall under the category of **impurity**, for instance, gluttony and intemperance.

Lust, evil desires. The two terms occur together in 1 Thessalonians 4:5. They also appear in a passage closely resembling the text, Galatians 5:24. The same vice may be viewed as a **lust** from its passive side and an "evil desire" from its active side. Here, if anything, **evil desires** is broader than **lust.** While **lust** includes all ungovernable affections, **evil desires** reaches to all evil longings.

And greed. "And (especially) covetousness." Impurity and greed may be said to include between them nearly the whole realm of human selfishness and vice.

Which is idolatry. Compare Ephesians 5:5. The covetous person sets up another object of worship besides God. There is a sort of religious purpose, the devotion of the soul to greed, which makes the sin of the miser so hateful. The idea of avarice as a religion may have been suggested to St. Paul by our Lord's words in Matthew 6:24, "You cannot serve both God and Money," though it is a mistake to suppose that Mammon was the name of a Syrian deity.

6. Coming. This may refer either to the present and continuous dispensation, or to the future and final judgment. The present "comes" is frequently used to denote the certainty of a future event (see Matthew 17:11; John 4:21).

7. In the life you once lived. When you lived in this atmosphere of sin, when you had not yet died to the world.

8. All such things as these. "Not only those vices which have been named before (verse 5) but all vices, of whatever kind." The apostle accordingly goes on to specify sins of a wholly different type from those already mentioned, sins of uncharitableness, such as anger, rage, malice, and the like.

Anger, rage. The one denotes a more or less settled feeling of hatred, the other a tumultuous outburst of passion.

Malice. Or "malignity," as it may be translated in default of a better word. This is not (at least in the New Testament) vice generally, but the vicious nature which is bent on doing harm to others. This is clear from the context in which it comes in Romans 1:29, Ephesians 4:31, and Titus 3:3. So **malice** and **sexual immorality** (verse 5) (which frequently occur together, for example in 1 Corinthians 5:8) only differ insofar as the one denotes the vicious disposition, the other the active exercise of it.

Slander. "Evil speaking, railing, slandering," as, for example, in Romans 3:8; 14:16; 1 Corinthians 4:13; 10:30; Ephesians 4:31; Titus 3:2.

9. Old self. As in Romans 6:6; Ephesians 4:22. With this expression compare Romans 7:22; 2 Corinthians 4:16; Ephesians 3:16; 1 Peter 3:4.

10. The new self. Compare Ephesians 4:24. The "new self" in these passages is not Christ himself but the regenerate person formed after Christ.

In knowledge. "Unto perfect knowledge," the true knowledge in Christ, as opposed to the false knowledge of the heretical teachers.

In the image of its Creator. The reference is to Genesis 1:26. See also Ephesians 4:24. This reference, however, does not imply an identity of the creation here mentioned with the creation of Genesis, but only an analogy between the two. The spiritual man in each believer's heart, like the primal man in the beginning of the world, was created after God's image. The new birth was a re-creation of God's image; the subsequent life must be a deepening of this image thus stamped on the man.

11. Here. That is, "in this regenerate life, in this spiritual region into which the believer is transferred in Christ."

No Greek or Jew. Comparing the enumeration here with the parallel passage in Galatians 3:28, we note the difference. In Galatians the abolition of all distinctions is stated in the broadest way by the selection of three typical instances: religious prerogative ("neither Jew nor Greek"), social caste ("slave nor free"), gender ("male nor female"). In Colossians, on the other hand, the examples are chosen with special reference to the immediate circumstances of the Colossian church. First, the Judaism of the Colossian heretics is met by **no Greek or Jew**, and as it manifested itself especially in enforcing circumcision, this is further emphasized by **circumcised or uncircumcised**. Second, their Gnosticism again is met by **no . . . barbarian, Scythian**. They laid special stress on intelligence and knowledge. The apostle offers the full privileges of the Gospel to barbarians. Third, special circumstances, connected with the eminent members of the church of Colosse, had directed Paul's attention at this moment to the relationship between masters and slaves. Hence he could not leave the subject without adding **slave or free**, though this has no special bearing on the Colossian heresy.

Circumcised. This enforces and extends the lesson of the previous clause. The abolition of distinctions applies to religious privilege, not only as inherited by birth (**Greek or Jew**), but also as assumed by adoption (**circumcised or uncircumcised**). It is no advantage to be born a Jew, and it is none to become a Jew; compare 1 Corinthians 7:19; Galatians 5:6; 6:15.

Barbarian. To the Jew, the whole world was divided into Jews and Greeks, the privileged and unprivileged sections of mankind, religious prerogative being taken as the line of demarcation. To the Greek and Roman, it was similarly divided into Greeks and barbarians, again the privileged and unprivileged sections of the human race, civilization and culture being now the criterion and distinction. Thus from the one point of view the Greek is contrasted disadvantageously with the Jew, while from the other he is contrasted advantageously with the barbarian. Both distinctions are equally antagonistic to the spirit of the Gospel. The apostle declares both null and void in Christ. The twofold character of the Colossian heresy enables him to strike at these two opposite forms of error with one blow.

The word **barbarian** correctly denoted one who spoke an inarticulate, stammering, unintelligible language. "Not till that word 'barbarian,'" writes Professor Max Müller, "was struck out of the dictionary of mankind and replaced by 'brother,' not until the right of all nations of the world to be classed as members of one genus or kind was recognized, can we look even for the first beginnings of our civilization. This change was effected by Christianity. . . . 'Humanity' is a word which you look for in vain in Plato or Aristotle; the idea of mankind as one family, as the children of one God, is an idea of Christian growth: and the science of mankind, and of the languages of mankind, is a science which, without Christianity, would never have sprung into life. When people had been taught to look on all men as brethren, then and only then, did the variety of human speech present itself as a problem that called for a solution in the eyes of thoughtful observers: and I therefore date the real beginning of the science of language from the first day of Pentecost."

St. Paul was the great exponent of the fundamental principle in the Christian church which was symbolized on the day of Pentecost when he declared, as here, that in Christ there is neither **Greek** nor **barbarian**, or as in Romans 1:14 that he himself was a debtor equally to "Greeks, and to Barbarians" (KJV).

Scythian. The lowest type of barbarian. The savageness of the Scythians was proverbial.

But Christ is all, and is in all. Christ has dispossessed and obliterated all distinctions of religious prerogative and intellectual preeminence and social

110

caste. Christ has substituted himself for all these. Christ occupies the whole sphere of human life and permeates all its developments; compare Ephesians 1:23.

12-15. Therefore, as God's chosen people, holy and dearly loved, clothe yourselves with compassion, kindness, humility, gentleness and patience. Bear with each other and forgive whatever grievances you may have against one another. Forgive as the Lord forgave you. And over all these virtues put on love, which binds them all together in perfect unity. Let the peace of Christ rule in your hearts, since as members of one body you were called to peace. And be thankful.

Therefore, as the elect of God, as a people consecrated to his service and specially endowed with his love, array yourselves in hearts of compassion, in kindliness and humility, in a gentle and yielding spirit. Bear with one another; forgive freely among yourselves. As your Master forgave you his servants, so ought you to forgive your fellow servants. And over all these robe yourselves in love; for this is the garment which binds together all the graces of perfection. And let the one supreme umpire in your hearts, the one referee in the middle of your difficulties, be the peace of Christ, which is the destined goal of your Christian calling, in which is realized the unity belonging to members of one body. Lastly, show your gratitude by your thanksgiving.

12. Therefore. As people to whom Christ has become all in all. The incidental mention of Christ (verse 11) as superseding all other relationships gives occasion to this argumentative **Therefore.** Compare 3:1.

As God's chosen people. "As elect ones of God." Compare Romans 8:23; Titus 1:1. With St. Paul the same people are called to Christ and chosen out of the world. St. Paul speaks of an individual Christian as "elect" or "chosen" (see Romans 16:13; 1 Corinthians 1:26-27; 1 Peter 1:1; 2 Peter 1:10).

Chosen denotes election by God not only to final salvation but to any special privilege or work, whether it be, first, to church membership (Romans 1:6-7), second, to the work of preaching (Acts 9:15), third, in Christ's case, the Messiahship (1 Peter 2:4, 6), fourth, in God's case, the Fatherhood of the chosen people (Romans 9:11), fifth, the faithful remnant under the theocracy (Romans 11:5, 7, 28).

Holy and dearly loved. These are not to be taken as vocatives but as predicates further defining the meaning of **chosen.** All three terms—**chosen, holy,** and **dearly loved**—are transferred from the old covenant to the new, from Israel after the flesh to Israel after the Spirit. For the two former see 1 Peter 2:9. For the third word, see Isaiah 5:1 and Hosea 2:23 (as quoted in Romans 9:25). In the New Testament it seems to be used always of the objects of God's love; for example, 1 Thessalonians 1:4; 2 Thessalonians 2:13. For the link between God's election and God's love see Romans 11:28.

111

Kindness, humility. These two words describe the disposition of the Christian mind in general. It affects either our relationship to others (**kindness**), or our estimate of self (**humility**).

Gentleness and patience. These next two words denote the exercise of the Christian temper in its outer bearing toward others. They are best distinguished by their opposites. **Gentleness** is the opposite of rudeness or harshness, while **patience** is the opposite of resentment, revenge, or wrath.

13. Grievances. "Grievances" are here regarded as debts which need to be remitted.

14. And over all these. "Over and above all these"; compare Luke 3:20. Love is the outer garment which holds the others in place.

Which binds them all together in perfect unity. "The bond of perfection," that is, the power which unites and holds together all those graces and virtues which together make up perfection.

15. The peace of Christ. "Christ's peace," which he left as a legacy to his disciples (see John 14:27; compare Ephesians 2:14).

Rule. "Umpire." Where there is a conflict of motives or desires, the peace of Christ must step in and decide which is to prevail.

Since as members of one body you were called to peace. "As you were called as members of one body, so let there be one spirit animating that body." This passage strikes the keynote of the companion letter to the Ephesians (see especially 2:14ff.; 4:3ff.).

16-17. Let the word of Christ dwell in you richly as you teach and admonish one another with all wisdom, and as you sing psalms, hymns and spiritual songs with gratitude in your hearts to God. And whatever you do, whether in word or deed, do it all in the name of the Lord Jesus, giving thanks to God the Father through him.

Let the inspiring word of Christ dwell in your hearts, enriching you with its boundless wealth and endowing you with all wisdom. Teach and admonish one another with psalms, with hymns of praise, with spiritual songs of all kinds. Only let them be pervaded with grace from heaven. Sing to God in your hearts and not with your lips only. And generally, whatever you do, whether in word or in deed, let everything be done in the name of Jesus Christ. And (again I repeat it) pour out your thanksgiving to God the Father through him.

16. The word of Christ. Here **of Christ** is the subjunctive genitive, so that Christ is the speaker. Though "the word of the Lord" and "the word of God" occur frequently, **the word of Christ** is found here only. There seems to be no direct reference in this expression to any definite body of truths either written or oral, but **the word of Christ** denotes the presence of Christ in the heart, as an inner monitor; compare 1 John 2:14.

Psalms, hymns and spiritual songs. The main idea of **psalms** is a musical accompaniment, and that of **hymns** praise to God, while **spiritual songs** is the general word for a song, whether accompanied or unaccompanied, whether of praise or on any other subject. Thus it was quite possible for a song to be at the same time a "psalm," a "hymn," and a "spiritual song."

In the text the reference to **psalms**, we may suppose, is especially, though not exclusively (1 Corinthians 14:26), to the psalms of David, which would in early times have formed part of the religious worship of the Christian brotherhood. On the other hand, **hymns** would more appropriately designate those hymns of praise which were composed by the Christians themselves on distinctly Christian themes, being either set forms of words or spontaneous effusions of the moment. The third term, **spiritual songs**, gathers up the other two and extends the precept to all forms of song, with the limitation however that they must be **spiritual**.

Psalmody and hymnody were highly developed in the religious services of the Jews at this time. They would thus find their way into the Christian church from the very beginning. For instances of singing hymns or psalms in the apostolic age, see Acts 4:24; 16:25; 1 Corinthians 14:15, 26. Hence even in St. Paul's letters, especially his later letters, fragments of such hymns appear to be quoted; for example, Ephesians 5:14.

The reference in the text is not solely or chiefly to public worship as such.

Sing . . . in your hearts to God. This external manifestation must be accompanied by the inner emotion. There must be the thanksgiving of the heart as well as of the lips; compare Ephesians 5:19.

17. In the name of the Lord Jesus. This is the great practical lesson which flows from the theological teaching of the letter. Hence the reiteration of **Lord** in verses 18, 20, 22, 23, 24.

Special Precepts (3:18—4:6)

The Obligations of Wives and Husbands, Children and Parents

18-21. Wives, submit to your husbands, as is fitting in the Lord. Husbands, love your wives and do not be harsh with them. Children, obey your parents in everything, for this pleases the Lord. Fathers, do not embitter your children, or they will become discouraged.

You wives, be subject to your husbands, for so it becomes you in Christ. You husbands, love and cherish your wives, and use no harshness toward them. You children, be obedient to your parents in all things, for this is commendable and lovely in Christ. You parents, vex not your children, lest they lose heart and grow sullen.

113

18ff. These precepts, providing for the conduct of Christians in private households, should be compared with Ephesians 5:22—6:9; 1 Peter 2:18—3:7; Titus 2:1ff.

20. In everything. The same in verse 22. The rule is stated absolutely because the exceptions are so few that they may be disregarded.

21. Do not embitter your children. Irritation is the first result of being too exacting with children, and irritation leads to moroseness (discouragement).

Become discouraged. "Lose heart, become spiritless," that is, go about their task in a listless, moody, sullen frame of mind.

The Obligations of Slaves and Masters

3:22—4:1. Slaves, obey your earthly masters in everything; and do it, not only when their eye is on you and to win their favor, but with sincerity of heart and reverence for the Lord. Whatever you do, work at it with all your heart, as working for the Lord, not for men, since you know that you will receive an inheritance from the Lord as a reward. It is the Lord Christ you are serving. Anyone who does wrong will be repaid for his wrong, and there is no favoritism. Masters, provide your slaves with what is right and fair, because you know that you also have a Master in heaven.

You slaves, be obedient in all things to the masters set over you in the flesh, not rendering them service only when their eyes are upon you, as aiming merely to please men, but serving in all sincerity of heart, as living in the sight of your heavenly Master and standing in awe of him. And in everything that you do, work faithfully and with all your soul, as laboring not for men, but for the great Lord and Master himself, knowing that you have a Master from whom you will receive the glorious inheritance as your recompense, whether or not you may be defrauded of your due by men. Yes, Christ is your Master, and you are his slaves. He that does a wrong shall be requited for his wrongdoing. I say not this of slaves only, but of masters also. There is no partiality, no respect of persons, in God's distribution of rewards and punishments. Therefore, you masters, do you also on your part deal justly and equitably by your slaves, knowing that you too have a Master in heaven.

22. Slaves. The relationship of masters and slaves, both here and in the companion letter (Ephesians 6:5-9), is treated at greater length than is usual with St. Paul. Here especially the expansion of this topic, compared with the brief space assigned to the duties of wives and husbands (verses 18-19) or of children and parents (verses 20-21), deserves to be noticed. The fact is explained by a contemporary incident in the apostle's private life. His connections with Onesimus had turned his thoughts in this direction.

When their eye is on you. "Eye-service," as in Ephesians 6:6. This happy expression would seem to be the apostle's own coinage. At least there are no traces of it earlier.

24. From the Lord. "However you may be treated by your earthly masters, you have still a Master who will recompense you."

An inheritance. There is a paradox involved in this word. Elsewhere the slave and the inheritance are contrasted (Matthew 21:35-38; Romans 8:15-17; Galatians 4:1, 7), but here the slave is the **inheritance**. This he is because though he is man's slave, he is "Christ's slave" (1 Corinthians 7:22), and thus "God has made you also an heir" (Galatians 4:7.)

25. Anyone who does wrong. There seems to be a double reference here. The warning is suggested by the case of the slave, but it is extended to the case of the master; this accords with the parallel passage, Ephesians 6:8.

The recent fault of Onesimus would make the apostle doubly anxious to emphasize the duties of the slave toward the master, lest in his love for the offender he should seem to condone the offense. This same word translated **does wrong** is used by St. Paul to describe the crime of Onesimus in Philemon 18. But on the other hand, it is the apostle's business to show that justice has a double edge. There must be a reciprocity between the master and the slave. The philosophers of Greece taught, and the laws of Rome assumed, that the slave was a chattel. But a chattel would have no rights. It would be absurd to talk of treating a chattel with justice. St. Paul places the relationship of the master and the slave in a wholly different light. Justice and equity are the expression of the divine mind; and with God there is **no favoritism**. With him the claims of the slave are as real as the claims of the master.

4:1. Right and fair. It seems a mistake to suppose that **fair** here has anything to do with the treatment of slaves as equals (compare Philemon 16). When linked with **right**, the word naturally suggests an even-handed, impartial treatment.

Provide. Here the idea is "reciprocation," the master's duty as corresponding to the slave's.

Have a Master. As in Ephesians 6:9; compare 1 Corinthians 7:22.

The Duty of Prayer and Thanksgiving and Right Behavior Toward the Unconverted (4:2-6)

2-6. Devote yourselves to prayer, being watchful and thankful. And pray for us, too, that God may open a door for our message, so that we may proclaim the mystery of Christ, for which I am in chains. Pray that I may proclaim it clearly, as I should. Be wise in the way you act toward outsiders; make the most of every opportunity. Let your conversation be always full of grace, seasoned with salt, so that you may know how to answer everyone.

Be earnest and unceasing in prayer; keep your hearts and minds awake while praying; remember also (as I have so often told you) that thanksgiving is the goal and crown of prayer. Meanwhile, in your petitions forget not us—myself Paul—my fellow laborer Timothy—your evangelist Epaphras—all the teachers of the Gospel. Pray that God may open a door for the preaching of the Word, to the end that we may proclaim the free offer of grace to the Gentiles—that great mystery of Christ for which I am now a prisoner in bonds. So shall I declare it fearlessly, as I am bound to proclaim it. Walk wisely and discreetly in all your dealings with unbelievers; allow no opportunity to slip through your hands, but buy up every passing moment. Let your language be always pervaded with grace and seasoned with salt. So will you know how to give a fit answer to each man, as the occasion demands.

2. Devote. "Cling closely to," "remain constant to" (compare Mark 3:9; Acts 8:13; 10:7), and so "continue steadfast in."

Watchful. Long continuance in prayer is apt to produce listlessness. Hence the additional charge that the heart must be awake if the prayer is to have any value. The word is not to be taken literally here but metaphorically.

Thankful. This is the crown of all prayer.

3. And pray for us. Here **us** is the apostles and preachers of the Gospel, with reference especially to Timothy (1:1) and Epaphras (4:12-13). When the apostle speaks of himself alone, he uses the singular (verses 3-4, **I am in chains** and **I may proclaim**).

Open a door for our message. "A door of admission for the word," that is, "an opportunity of preaching the Gospel," as in 1 Corinthians 16:9 and 2 Corinthians 2:12. The **message** here is the Gospel, as occurs frequently elsewhere.

The mystery of Christ. That is, the teaching of the free admission of the Gentiles. This is the leading idea which St. Paul in these letters attaches to **the mystery** of the Gospel; see 1:26-27.

For which. St. Paul might have been still at large if he had been content to preach a Judaic gospel. It was because he contended for Gentile liberty, and thus offended Jewish prejudices, that he found himself a prisoner. See Acts 21:28; 22:21-22; 24:5-6; 25:6, 8.

In chains. See 2 Timothy 2:9 and Philemon 10.

4. Pray that I may proclaim. The immediate purport of the Colossians' prayers must be that the apostle should have opportunities for preaching the Gospel, the ulterior object being that he should use those opportunities boldly.

5. Outsiders. "Those outside the pale" of the church, unbelievers, as in

1 Corinthians 5:12-13 and 1 Thessalonians 4:12. See also 1 Timothy 3:7. The believers, on the other hand, are "those inside" (1 Corinthians 5:12).

Make the most of every opportunity. "Buying up the opportunity for yourselves," letting no opportunity slip away to say and do what may further God's cause. Compare Ephesians 5:16, where the reason for the injunction is added: "because the days are evil." The prevailing evil of the times makes the opportunities for good more precious.

6. Full of grace. "With grace, favor," that is, "acceptableness," "pleasingness"; compare Ecclesiastes 10:12.

Seasoned with salt. Compare Mark 9:50. Salt has two uses. First, it gives a flavor to the discourse and recommends it to the palate; compare Job 6:6. This is the primary idea of the metaphor here, as the word **seasoned** seems to indicate. Second, salt preserves from corruption and renders wholesome.

Everyone. The apostle's precept was enforced by his own example, for he made it a rule to "become all things to all men so that by all possible means I might save some" (1 Corinthians 9:22).

Colossians 4:7-18

Explanations About the Letter (4:7-9)

7-9. Tychicus will tell you all the news about me. He is a dear brother, a faithful minister and fellow servant in the Lord. I am sending him to you for the express purpose that you may know about our circumstances and that he may encourage your hearts. He is coming with Onesimus, our faithful and dear brother, who is one of you. They will tell you everything that is happening here.

You will learn everything about me from Tychicus, the beloved brother who has ministered to me and served with me faithfully in the Lord. This indeed was my purpose in sending him to you: that you might be informed how matters stand with me, and that he might cheer your hearts and strengthen your resolves by those tidings. Onesimus will accompany him— a faithful and beloved brother, who is one of yourselves, a Colossian. Those two will inform you of all that is going on here.

7. Tychicus. Tychicus was charged by St. Paul at this same time with a more extended mission. He was entrusted with copies of the circular letter, which he was told to deliver to the principal churches of proconsular Asia. This mission would bring him to Laodicea, which was one of the great centers of Christianity; as Colosse was only a few miles away, the apostle would naturally engage him to pay a visit to the Colossians. At the same time the presence of an authorized delegate of St. Paul, as Tychicus was known to be, would serve to recommend Onesimus who, owing to his former conduct, stood in every need of such a recommendation.

Tychicus was born in proconsular Asia (Acts 20:4) and is also associated with Ephesus (2 Timothy 4:12). He is found with St. Paul at three different epochs of his life. First, he accompanied the apostle on his way eastward at the close of the third missionary journey A.D. 58 (Acts 20:4) and probably, like Trophimus (Acts 21:29), went with him to Jerusalem. It is probable that Tychicus, together with others mentioned among St. Paul's numerous retinue on this occasion, was a delegate appointed by his own church according to the apostle's injunctions (1 Corinthians 16:3-4) to bear the contributions of his brethren to the poor Christians of Judea; and if so, he may possibly be the person recommended as the brother "who is praised by all the churches for his service to the gospel" (2 Corinthians 8:18), though this depends on the interpretation of Acts 20:5.

Second, we find Tychicus again in St. Paul's company at the time with which we are immediately concerned, when this letter was written, probably toward the end of the first Roman captivity. Third, at the close of St. Paul's life (about A.D. 67), Tychicus appears to have again associated himself with the apostle, his name being mentioned in connection with a mission to Crete (Titus 3:12) and another to Ephesus (2 Timothy 4:12).

Minister. But to whom? To the churches or to St. Paul himself? The following phrase, **fellow servant**, suggests the latter as the prominent idea here. So in Acts 19:22 Timothy and Erastus are described as "two of his helpers." Tychicus himself also was one of several who ministered to St. Paul about that time (Acts 20:4). It is not probable, however, that **minister** has here its strict official sense, "a deacon," as in Romans 16:1; Philippians 1:1; 1 Timothy 3:8, 12.

Fellow servant. The word does not occur elsewhere in St. Paul, except in 1:7, where it is used of Epaphras. It is probably owing to the fact of St. Paul's applying the term in both these passages to people whom he calls "ministers" that **fellow servant** seems to have been adopted as a customary form of address in the early church on the part of a bishop when speaking of a deacon.

8. That he may encourage your hearts. That is, "encourage you to persevere by his tidings and exhortations." The phrase occurs again in Ephesians 6:22 and 2 Thessalonians 2:17. The prominent idea in all these passages is not comfort or consolation but perseverance in the right way.

9. Our faithful and dear brother. The man whom the Colossians had only known up to then, if they knew him at all, as a worthless runaway slave is thus commended to them as no more a slave but a brother, no more dishonest and faithless but trustworthy, no more an object of contempt but of love; compare Philemon 11, 16.

Greetings from Different People (4:10-14)

10-14. My fellow prisoner Aristarchus sends you his greetings, as does Mark, the cousin of Barnabas. (You have received instructions about him; if he comes to you, welcome him.) Jesus, who is called Justus, also sends greetings. These are the only Jews among my fellow workers for the kingdom of God, and they have proved a comfort to me. Epaphras, who is one of you and a servant of Christ Jesus, sends greetings. He is always wrestling in prayer for you, that you may stand firm in all the will of God, mature and fully assured. I vouch for him that he is working hard for you and for those at Laodicea and Hierapolis. Our dear friend Luke, the doctor, and Demas send greetings.

I send you greeting from Aristarchus who is a fellow prisoner with me; from Marcus, Barnabas' cousin, concerning whom I have already sent you directions, that you welcome him heartily if he pays you a visit; and from Jesus, surnamed Justus; all three Hebrew converts. They alone of their fellow countrymen have worked loyally with me in spreading the kingdom of God; and their steadfastness has indeed been a comfort to me in the hour of trial. Greeting also from Epaphras, your fellow townsman, a true servant of Christ, who is ever wrestling in his prayers on your behalf, that you may stand firm in the faith, perfectly instructed and fully convinced in every will and purpose of God. I bear testimony to the earnestness with which he labors for you and the brethren of Laodicea and those of Hierapolis. Greeting also from Luke the physician, my very dear friend, and from Demas.

10. The greetings to Philemon (Philemon 23-24) are sent from the same people as to the Colossians, except that in the former case the name Jesus Justus is omitted.

Aristarchus. The Thessalonian started with St. Paul on his voyage from Jerusalem to Rome but probably had parted from the apostle at Myra. If so, he must have rejoined him at Rome at a later date. He would be well-known in proconsular Asia, which he had visited from time to time (Acts 19:29; 20:4; 27:2).

Fellow prisoner. In Philemon 23 this honorable title is withheld from Aristarchus and given to Epaphras. In Romans 16:7 St. Paul's relatives Andronicus and Junias are called by this name.

Mark. This is doubtless John Mark, who had been associated with St. Paul in his earlier missionary work (Acts 12:25; 15:37ff.). This commendatory notice is especially interesting as being the first mention of him since the separation some twelve years before (Acts 15:39). In the later years of the apostle's life he entirely effaced the unfavorable impression left by Mark's earlier desertion (2 Timothy 4:11).

This notice is likewise important for two other reasons. First, Mark appears here as commended to a church of proconsular Asia and intending to visit those parts. To the churches of the same region he sends a greeting in 1 Peter 5:13; and he is apparently found in this district a few years later (2 Timothy 4:11). Second, Mark is now residing at Rome. His link with the metropolis appears also from 1 Peter 5:13, if "Babylon" there (as seems most probable) is correctly interpreted as Rome; and early tradition speaks of his gospel as having been written for the Romans.

The cousin. The term **cousin** is applied to cousins in general, whether the children of two brothers or of two sisters or of a brother and sister. There is no reason to suppose that St. Paul would or could have used this in any other than its correct sense. St. Mark's relationship with Barnabas may have been through his mother Mary, who is mentioned in Acts 12:12. The incidental notice here explains why Barnabas should have taken a more favorable view of Mark's defection than St. Paul (Acts 15:37-39).

The notices in this passage and in 2 Timothy 4:11 show that Mark had recovered the apostle's good opinion. The studious recommendation of St. Mark in both passages indicates a desire to efface the unfavorable impression of the past.

The name Mark occurs in five different settings, first as the early disciple, John Mark, Acts 12:12, 25; 15:39; second, as the later companion to St. Paul, here and in Philemon 24; 2 Timothy 4:11; third, as the companion and "son" of St. Peter, 1 Peter 5:13; fourth, as the evangelist; fifth, as the bishop of Alexandria. The scriptural notices suggest that the same Mark is intended in all the occurrences of the name, for they are connected together by personal links (Peter, Paul, Barnabas); and the earliest forms of tradition likewise identify him.

Barnabas. Whenever St. Paul mentions Barnabas after the collision at Antioch (Galatians 2:11ff.) and the separation of missionary spheres (Acts 15:39), he does so in affectionate tones.

You have received instructions about him. These injunctions must have been communicated previously either by letter or by word of mouth. The natural inference is that they were sent by St. Paul himself and not by anyone else, for example by St. Peter or St. Barnabas, as some have suggested. Thus the notice points to earlier communications between the apostle and Colosse.

11. Jesus. He is not mentioned elsewhere. Even in the letter to Philemon his name is omitted. Probably he was not a man of any prominence in the church, but his personal devotion to the apostle prompted this honorable mention.

Justus. A common name or surname of Jews and proselytes, denoting obedience and devotion to the law. It is applied to two people in the New Testament, besides this Justus—first, to Joseph Barsabbas (Acts 1:23), second, to a proselyte at Corinth (Acts 18:7).

12. Epaphras. His full name would have been Epaphroditus, but he is always called by the shortened form Epaphras and must not be confused with the Philippian Epaphroditus who also was with St. Paul at one period of his Roman captivity.

Who is one of you. "Who belongs to you," that is, he was born at

Colosse or was at least living at Colosse, as in the case of Onesimus (verse 9); compare Acts 4:6; 21:8; Romans 16:10-11; 1 Corinthians 12:16; Philippians 4:22.

A servant of Christ Jesus. This title, which the apostle uses several times of himself, is not elsewhere conferred on any other individual, except once on Timothy (Philippians 1:1), and probably points to exceptional service in the cause of the Gospel on the part of Epaphras.

Wrestling. Compare Romans 15:30. See also the great "wrestling" prayer in Luke 22:44.

Fully assured. "Fully persuaded." This verb has several meanings. First, "to fulfill, accomplish" (2 Timothy 4:5); second, "to persuade fully, to convince" (Romans 4:21); and, third, "to fill" (Romans 15:13). Here it should be translated "fulfilled, accomplished."

13. And for those at Laodicea and Hierapolis. The neighboring cities are taken in geographical order, starting from Colosse. Epaphras, though a Colossian, may have been the evangelist of the two larger cities also.

14. Our dear friend Luke. St. Luke had traveled with St. Paul on his previous journey to Jerusalem (Acts 21:1ff.). He had also accompanied him two years later from Jerusalem to Rome (Acts 27:2ff.). And now again, probably after another interval of two years, we find him in the apostle's company. It is not probable that he remained with St. Paul in the meanwhile, and this will account for his name not occurring in the letter to the Philippians. He was at the apostle's side in his second captivity (2 Timothy 4:11).

The doctor. Indications of medical knowledge have been traced both in the third gospel and in the Acts of the Apostles. It has been observed also that St. Luke's first appearance in company with St. Paul (Acts 16:10) nearly synchronizes with an attack of the apostle's constitutional illness (Galatians 4:13-14); so he may have joined him partly in a professional capacity. This conjecture is perhaps borne out by the personal feeling which breathes in the phrase, **our dear friend**. Whatever may be thought of these points, there is no ground for questioning the ancient belief that the physician is also the evangelist. St. Paul's motive in specifying him as **the doctor** may not have been to distinguish him from any other bearing the same name but to emphasize his own obligations to his medical knowledge. The name in this form does not appear to have been common. The tradition that St. Luke was a painter is quite late. It is worth noting that the two evangelists are mentioned together in this context, as also in Philemon 24 and 2 Timothy 4:11.

Demas. While Luke is described with special tenderness as **our dear friend ... the doctor**, Demas is dismissed with a bare mention and without any epithet of commendation.

A Message to Laodicea (4:15-17)

*15-17. Give my greetings to the brothers at Laodicea, and to Nympha
and the church in her house. After this letter has been read to you, see that
it is also read in the church of the Laodiceans and that you in turn read
the letter from Laodicea. Tell Archippus: "See to it that you complete the
work you have received in the Lord."*

*Greet from me the brethren who are in Laodicea, especially Nympha and
the church which assembles in her house. And when this letter has been
read among you, take care that it is read also in the church of the
Laodiceans, and be sure that you also read the letter which I have sent to
Laodicea and which you will get from them. Moreover, give this message
from me to Archippus: Take heed to the ministry which you have received
from me in Christ, and discharge it fully and faithfully.*

15. Nympha. As the context shows, an inhabitant of Laodicea. The
name in full would probably be Nymphodorus, as Artemas (Titus 3:12) for
Artemidorus, Zenas (Titus 3:13) for Zenodorus, Theudas (Acts 5:36) for
Theodorus, Olympas (Romans 16:15) for Olympiodorus, and probably
Hermas (Romans 16:14) for Hermodorus.

The church in her house. The same expression is used of Prisca and
Aquila both at Rome (Romans 16:5) and at Ephesus (1 Corinthians 16:19),
and also of Philemon (Philemon 2). The Christians were first recognized
by the Roman government as "*collegia*" or burial clubs and, protected by
this recognition, doubtless held their meetings for religious worship. There
is no clear example of a separate building set apart for Christian worship
within the limits of the Roman Empire before the third century, though
apartments in private houses might be specially devoted to this purpose.

16. This letter. The letter which has just been concluded, for these greetings have the character of a postscript; compare Romans 16:22 and
2 Thessalonians 3:14.

See that it is also read in the church of the Laodiceans. A similar
charge is given in 1 Thessalonians 5:27. The precaution here is probably
suggested by the distastefulness of the apostle's warnings, which might lead
to the suppression of the letter.

You in turn read the letter from Laodicea. That is, "the letter left at
Laodicea, which you will procure from there."

There are good reasons for the belief that St. Paul here alludes to the so-
called letter to the Ephesians, which was in fact a circular letter addressed
to the principal churches of proconsular Asia. Tychicus was obliged to pass
through Laodicea on his way to Colosse and would leave a copy there
before the Colossian letter was delivered.

17. Tell Archippus. Why does not the apostle address himself directly to

Archippus? It might be answered that he probably thought the warning would come with greater emphasis when delivered by the voice of the church. Some also claim that perhaps Archippus was not resident at Colosse but at Laodicea.

The work. From the emphasis that is put on this word, the **work** here would seem to refer, as in the case of Tychicus (verse 7), to some higher function than the diaconate. In Acts 12:25 the same phrase is used of a temporary ministry, the collection and transporting of the alms for the poor of Jerusalem (Acts 11:29-30); but the solemnity of the warning here points to a continuous office rather than an immediate service.

Farewell (4:18)

18. I, Paul, write this greeting in my own hand. Remember my chains. Grace be with you.

I add this salutation with my own hand, signing it with my name Paul. Be mindful of my bonds. God's grace be with you.

18. Greeting. The letter was evidently written by an amanuensis (compare Romans 16:22). The final greeting, along with the accompanying sentence **Remember my chains . . .**, was in the apostle's own handwriting. This seems to have been the apostle's general practice, even where he does not call attention to his own signature. In 2 Thessalonians 3:17ff. and 1 Corinthians 16:21, as here, he directs his readers' notice to the fact, but in other letters he is silent. In some cases, however, he writes much more than the final sentence. Thus the whole letter to Philemon is apparently in his own handwriting (see Philemon 19), and in the letter to the Galatians he writes a long paragraph at the close.

Chains. His bonds establish an additional claim to a hearing. He who is suffering for Christ has a right to speak on behalf of Christ. The appeal is similar in Ephesians 3:1, which is resumed again (after a long digression) in Ephesians 4:1; so, too, Philemon 9. These passages seem to show that the appeal here is not for himself but for his teaching—not for sympathy with his sufferings but for obedience to the Gospel. His bonds were not his own; they were "for the gospel" (Philemon 13). See also Galatians 6:17.

Grace be with you. This very short form of the final benediction appears only here and in 1 Timothy 6:21; 2 Timothy 4:22. In Titus 3:15 "all" is inserted, and likewise in Hebrews 13:25.

PHILEMON

Introduction

The letter to Philemon holds a unique place among St. Paul's writings. It is the only strictly private letter which has been preserved. The Pastoral Letters indeed are addressed to individuals, but they discuss important matters of church discipline and government. Evidently they were intended to be read by others besides those to whom they were immediately addressed. On the other hand, the letter to Philemon does not once mention any question of public interest. It is addressed apparently to a layman. It is wholly occupied with an incident of domestic life. The occasion which called it forth was altogether commonplace. It is only one sample of countless letters which must have been written to many friends and disciples by one of St. Paul's eager temperament and warm affections in the course of a long and checkered life. Yet, for us this fragment which has been rescued from the wreck of a large and varied correspondence is infinitely precious. Nowhere is the social influence of the Gospel more strikingly exerted, nowhere does the nobility of the apostle's character receive a more vivid illustration than in this pleading on behalf of a runaway slave.

The People Written to

The letter introduces us to an ordinary household in a small town in Phrygia. Four members of it are mentioned by name—the father, the mother, the son, and the slave.

Philemon

The head of the family bears a name which, for good or for evil, was not unknown in connection with Phrygian history. The legend of Philemon and Baucis, the elderly peasants who entertained not angels but gods unawares and were rewarded by their divine guests for their warm hospitality and their conjugal love, is one of the most attractive in Greek mythology and contrasts favorably with many a revolting tale in which the powers of Olympus are represented as visiting this lower earth. It has a special interest too for the apostolic history because it suggests an explanation of the scene at Lystra when the barbarians would have sacrificed to the apostles, imagining that they were two gods, Zeus and Hermes, who had once again deigned to visit them in the form of men.

Again we read from history of one Philemon who obtained an unenviable notoriety at Athens by assuming the rights of Athenian citizenship, though a Phrygian and apparently a slave. Otherwise the name is not distinctively Phrygian. It does not occur with any special frequency in the inscriptions in that country, and though several people bearing this name became famous in literary history, not one, so far as we know, was a Phrygian.

The Philemon with whom we are concerned was born, or at least lived, in Colosse. This is seen by the fact that his slave is mentioned as belonging to that place. It may be added, to confirm this view, that in one of two letters written and sent at the same time, St. Paul announces the restoration of Onesimus to his master, while in the other he speaks of this same person as revisiting Colosse (compare Colossians 4:9 with Philemon 11ff.).

Philemon had been converted by St. Paul himself (verse 19). When and under what circumstances he received his first lessons in the Gospel, we do not know. But the apostle's long stay in Ephesus naturally suggests itself as the time when he was most likely to have met with a citizen of Colosse.

Philemon proved worthy of his spiritual heritage. Though to Epaphras belongs the chief glory of preaching the Gospel at Colosse, his labors are well seconded by Philemon. The title of **fellow worker** (verse 1), conferred on him by the apostle, is a noble testimony to his evangelical zeal. Like Nympha in the neighboring church of Laodicea (Colossians 4:15), Philemon had placed his house at the disposal of the Christians at Colosse for their religious and social meetings (verse 2). Like Gaius (3 John 5ff.), to whom the only other private letter in the apostolic canon is written (assuming that 2 John is written to a church), he was generous with his hospitality. All those with whom he came into contact spoke with gratitude about his kindly attentions (verses 5, 7). Of his subsequent career we have no certain knowledge. Legendary story indeed promotes him to the bishopric of Colosse and records how he was martyred in his native city under Nero. But this tradition or fiction is not entitled to any credit. All that we really know of Philemon is contained within this letter itself.

Apphia, the Wife

It is a safe inference from the link between the names that Apphia was the wife of Philemon. From the overwhelming evidence of inscriptions, it is impossible to doubt that Apphia is a native Phrygian name. Of this Phrygian matron we know nothing more than can be gleaned from this letter. The tradition or fiction which depicts her being martyred with her husband may be safely discarded. St. Paul addresses her as a Christian (**our sister**, verse 2). Equally with her husband she had been aggrieved by the misconduct of their slave Onesimus, and equally with him she might interest herself in the penitent's future well-being.

Archippus, the Son

With less confidence, but still with a reasonable degree of probability, we may infer that Archippus, who is also mentioned in the opening greeting, was a son of Philemon and Apphia. Archippus held some important office in the church (Colossians 4:17). St. Paul talks of it as a "work," "ministry" (*diakonia*). He speaks of Archippus as **our fellow soldier** in verse 2. Archippus may have been a presbyter. Or perhaps he held a missionary charge and belonged to the order of "evangelists" (see Ephesians 4:11).

Another question arises about Archippus: where did he exercise his ministry, whatever it was? At Colosse or at Laodicea? His link with Philemon would suggest the former place. But in the letter to the Colossians his name is mentioned immediately after the greeting to the Laodiceans and the directions affecting that church; and this seems to link him with Laodicea. On the whole this seems to be the more probable solution. Laodicea was within walking distance of Colosse. Archippus must have been in constant touch with his parents, who lived there; and it was therefore quite natural that, writing to the father and mother, St. Paul should mention the son's name also in the opening address, though he was not on the spot. We know nothing of his later life.

Onesimus

But far more important to the history of Christianity than the parents or the son of the family is the servant. The name Onesimus was very common among slaves. Like other words meaning "utility," "worth," and so on, it naturally lent itself to this purpose. Onesimus represented the least respectable class in the social scale. He was regarded by philosophers as live chattel, a living implement. He was treated in law as having no rights. He was now also a thief and a runaway. Rome was the natural cesspool for thee offscourings of humanity. In the dregs of the city rabble was his best hope of secrecy.

His Encounter with St. Paul in Rome. But in Rome the apostle spread his net for him, and Onesimus was caught in its meshes. Whatever motive may have drawn him to the apostle's side—whether the pangs of hunger or the gnawings of conscience—when he was in his grip, he could not escape. He listened, was impressed, was convinced, was baptized. The slave of Philemon became the free man in Christ (1 Corinthians 7:22). St. Paul found not only a sincere convert but a devoted friend in his latest son in the faith. For St. Paul the conventional barrier between slave and free had completely vanished before the dissolving presence of an eternal truth (1 Corinthians 7:21ff.; Galatians 3:28; Colossians 3:11). St. Paul found in Onesimus something more than a slave—a beloved brother, both as a slave and as a man, **both as a man and as a brother in the Lord** (verse 16). To take away Onesimus was to tear out St. Paul's heart (verse 12).

But there was a pressing reason for this sacrifice. Onesimus had repented, but he had not made restitution. He could only do this by submitting again to the servitude from which he had escaped. Philemon must be made to feel that when Onesimus was won for Christ, he was won back to his old master as well. But if the claim of duty demanded a great sacrifice from Paul, it demanded a greater still from Onesimus. By returning he would place himself entirely at the mercy of the master whom he had wronged. Roman law, more cruel than Athenian, gave limitless powers to a master over his slave. Life or death remained in Philemon's hands. Slaves were constantly crucified for far smaller offenses than his. As a thief and a runaway he had no claim to forgiveness.

The Mediation of Tychicus. A favorable opportunity occurred for restoring Onesimus to his master. Tychicus, as the bearer of letters from the apostle to Laodicea and Colosse, had reason to visit those parts. He could undertake the office of mediator and plead the cause of the penitent slave with the offended master. Under his shelter Onesimus would be safer than if he encountered Philemon alone. But St. Paul is not satisfied with this precaution. He will with his own hand write a few words of eager, affectionate entreaty, identifying himself with the cause of Onesimus. So he takes up his pen.

Analysis of the Letter

After the opening greetings to Philemon and the members of his family, St. Paul expresses his gratitude for the report which has reached his ears about his friend's charitable deeds. It is a great joy and encouragement to the apostle that so many brethren have had reason to bless Philemon's name. This widespread reputation for kindness makes him bold enough to reveal his purpose in writing. Though he has a right to command, he prefers to entreat. He has a petition to ask on behalf of a child of his own. This is none other than Onesimus, whom Philemon will remember only as a worthless creature, altogether untrue to his name, but who now is a reformed man. Paul wanted to keep Onesimus, for he could ill afford to dispense with his loving services. Indeed Philemon would doubtless have been glad thus to minister to the apostle's needs. But a benefit which has the appearance of being forced, whether truly so or not, loses all its value, and therefore the apostle sends the slave back. Indeed, there may have been in this desertion a divine providence. Onesimus may have been withheld from Philemon for a time, that he might be restored to him forever. He may have left as a slave, that he might return more than a slave. To others—to the apostle himself especially—he is now a dearly beloved brother. Must he not be this and more than this to Philemon, whether in earthly things or in heavenly things?

St. Paul therefore begs Philemon to receive Onesimus as he would receive himself. As for any injury that he may have done, as for any money that he may owe, the apostle makes himself responsible for this. The present letter may be accepted as a bond, a security for repayment. Yet at the same time he cannot refrain from reminding Philemon that he might fairly claim the remission of so small an amount. Does not his friend owe him his own soul? Yes, he has a right to look for some filial gratitude and duty from one to whom he stands as a spiritual father. Philemon will surely not refuse him this comfort in his many trials. St. Paul writes in the full confidence that he will be obeyed; he is quite sure that his friend will do more than is asked of him. At the same time he trusts to see him before very long, to talk over this and other matters. Philemon may provide him a lodging, for he hopes through their prayers that he may be liberated and given back to them. Then follow the greetings, and the letter ends with the apostle's blessing.

The Result of the Appeal

Of the result of this appeal we have no definite knowledge. It is reasonable to suppose, however, that Philemon would not dash the apostle's hopes, and that he would receive the slave back as a brother, and that he would even go further and meet the exact terms of St. Paul's petition and emancipate the penitent. But all this is mere conjecture.

Christianity and Slavery

The Gospel never directly attacks slavery as an institution; the apostles never command the liberation of slaves as an absolute duty. It is a remarkable fact that St. Paul in this letter stops short of any positive injunction. The word "emancipation" seems to be trembling on his lips, and yet he does not once utter it. He charges Philemon to take the runaway slave Onesimus into his confidence again, to receive him with all affection, to regard him no more as a slave but as a brother, to treat him with the same consideration, the same love, which he entertains for the apostle himself, to whom he owes everything. In fact, he tells him to do very much more than emancipate his slave, but this one thing he does not directly command. St. Paul's treatment of this individual case is an apt illustration of the attitude of Christianity toward slavery in general.

Commentary

Where the Spirit of the Lord is, there is liberty.
Who is weak, and I am not weak?
Who is offended, and I burn not?

Such ever was love's way: to rise, it stoops.

1-3. Paul, a prisoner of Christ Jesus, and Timothy our brother, To Philemon our dear friend and fellow worker, to Apphia our sister, to Archippus our fellow soldier and to the church that meets in your home: Grace to you and peace from God our Father and the Lord Jesus Christ.

Paul, now a prisoner of Christ Jesus, and Timothy, to Philemon, our dearly-beloved and fellow laborer in the Gospel, and to Apphia our sister, and to Archippus our fellow soldier in Christ, and to the church which assembles in your home. Grace and peace to you all from God our Father and the Lord Jesus Christ.

1. Prisoner. The authoritative title of "apostle" is dropped because throughout this letter St. Paul desires to entreat rather than to command (see verses 8-9). In its place is put a designation which would touch his friend's heart. How could Philemon resist an appeal which was penned within prison walls and by a chained hand?

Timothy. Timothy seems to have been with St. Paul during a great part of his three years' stay in Ephesus (Acts 19:22) and could hardly have failed to make the acquaintance of Philemon.

Fellow worker. It was probably during St. Paul's long stay at Ephesus that Philemon labored with him.

2. Fellow soldier. The spiritual campaigns in which **Archippus** was his comrade probably took place while St. Paul was at Ephesus (A.D. 54-57).

4-7. I always thank my God as I remember you in my prayers, because I hear about your faith in the Lord Jesus and your love for all the saints. I pray that you may be active in sharing your faith, so that you will have a full understanding of every good thing we have in Christ. Your love has given me great joy and encouragement, because you, brother, have refreshed the hearts of the saints.

I never cease to give thanks to my God for your well-doing, and you are always mentioned in my prayers. For others tell me of your love and faith—your faith which you have in the Lord Jesus, and your love which you show toward all the saints; and it is my prayer that this active sympathy and charity, thus springing from your faith, may abound more and more as you attain to the perfect knowledge of every good thing bestowed on us by God, looking to and striving after Christ. For indeed it gave me great joy and comfort to hear of your loving-kindness and to learn how the hearts of God's people have been cheered and refreshed by your help, my dear brother.

4-7. The apostle's thanksgiving and intercessory prayer (verse 4)—the reason for his thanksgiving (verse 5)—the subject of his prayer (verse 6)—the joy and comfort which he has in Philemon's good deeds (verse 7)—this is the very simple order of topics in these verses.

4. I remember you in my prayers. Here **remember** involves the idea of intercession on behalf of Philemon.

5. Because I hear about. This information would probably come from Epaphras (Colossians 1:7-8; 4:12) rather than from Onesimus.

Your faith in the Lord Jesus and your love for all the saints. That is, "the faith which you have toward the Lord Jesus Christ and the love which you show to all the saints." [In the KJV] the clauses are inverted in the second part of the sentence, thus producing an example of the figure called chiasm (see Galatians 4:4-5). This results here from the apostle's setting down the thoughts in the sequence in which they occur to him without paying regard to symmetrical arrangement. The first and prominent thought is Philemon's love. This suggests the mention of his faith as the source from which it springs. This again requires a reference to the object of faith. And then at last comes the deferred sequel to the first thought—the range and comprehensiveness of his love. The transition from the object of faith to the object of love is easier because the love is represented as springing from faith.

6. In sharing your faith. Of the many interpretations offered, two seem to deserve attention. First, "Your friendly offices and sympathies, your kindly deeds of charity, which spring from your faith." The idea of sharing, both one's faith and one's possessions, is a recurring one in the New Testament letters (Philippians 1:5; Hebrews 13:16; Romans 15:26, 2

Corinthians 8:4; 9:13). Second, "Your communion with God through faith"; compare 1 Corinthians 1:9, and see also 1 John 1:3, 6-7. The parallel passages strongly support the former sense.

A full understanding. This **understanding,** involving as it does the complete appropriation of all truth and unreserved identification with God's will, is the goal and crown of the believer's course. The apostle does not say "in the possession" or "in the performance" but in the **understanding of every good thing,** for in this higher sense of knowledge, to know is both to possess and to perform. The **understanding** which the apostle contemplates is Philemon's own.

We have in Christ. "Which is placed within our reach by the Gospel"; that is, the whole range of spiritual blessings, the complete cycle of Christian truth.

In Christ. That is, leading to him as the goal.

7. Joy. This sentence again must not be linked with the words immediately preceding. It gives the motive of the apostle's thanksgiving mentioned in verse 4. This thanksgiving was the outpouring of gratitude for the joy and comfort that he had received in his bonds from the report of Philemon's generous charity.

The hearts. The heart was thought of as the seat of the emotions.

Refreshed. Compare verse 20. This compound expresses a temporary relief. Thus it implies "relaxation, refreshment" as a preparation for the renewal of labor or suffering.

8-17. Therefore, although in Christ I could be bold and order you to do what you ought to do, yet I appeal to you on the basis of love. I then, as Paul—an old man and now also a prisoner of Christ Jesus—I appeal to you for my son Onesimus, who became my son while I was in chains. Formerly he was useless to you, but now he has become useful both to you and to me. I am sending him—who is my very heart—back to you. I would have liked to keep him with me so that he could take your place in helping me while I am in chains for the gospel. But I did not want to do anything without your consent, so that any favor you do will be spontaneous and not forced. Perhaps the reason he was separated from you for a little while was that you might have him back for good—no longer as a slave, but better than a slave, as a dear brother. He is very dear to me but even dearer to you, both as a man and as a brother in the Lord. So if you consider me a partner, welcome him as you would welcome me.

Encouraged by these tidings of your loving spirit, I prefer to entreat where I might command. My office gives me authority to dictate your duty in plain language, but love bids me plead as a suitor. Have I not indeed a right to command—I Paul whom Christ Jesus long ago commissioned as

*his ambassador and whom now he has exalted to the rank of his prisoner?
But I entreat you. I have a favor to ask for a son of my own—one doubly
dear to me because I became his father in the middle of the sorrows of my
bonds. I speak of Onesimus, who in times past was found wholly untrue to
his name, who was then far from useful to you, but now is useful to you—
yes, and to me also. Him I send back to you, and I entreat you to take him
in your favor, for in giving him I am giving my own heart. Indeed I would
gladly have detained him with me, that he might minister to me on your
behalf in these bonds with which the Gospel has invested me. But I had
scruples. I did not wish to do anything without your direct consent; for then
it might have seemed (though it were only seeming) as if your kindly offices
had been given by compulsion and not of free will. So I have sent him
back. Indeed it may have been God's providential design that he was
parted from you for a season, only that you might regain him forever; that
he left you as a slave, only that he might return to you a beloved brother.
This indeed he is to me most of all; and if to me, must he not be so much
more to thee, both in worldly things and in spiritual? If therefore you
regard me as a friend and companion, take him to yourself as if he were me.*

8. Therefore. That is, "Seeing that I have proofs of your love, I prefer to
entreat, where I might command."

I could be bold. "Confidence," literally "freedom" or "privilege of
speech." It was his apostolic authority which gave him this right to command in plain language. Hence the addition of **in Christ**.

9. On the basis of love. That is, "having respect to the claims of love."
It is not Philemon's love (verses 5, 7), nor St. Paul's own love, but love
absolutely, love regarded as a principle which demands a deferential
respect.

As Paul. The mention of his personal name involves an assertion of
authority, as in Ephesians 3:1; compare Galatians 5:2.

A prisoner. Another title to respect. The mention of his bonds might
suggest either an appeal for commiseration or a claim of authority. Here the
addition of **Christ Jesus** invests it with the character of an official title and
so gives prominence to the latter idea. To his old office of "ambassador"
Christ has added the new title of **prisoner**.

10. I appeal to you. So, too, 1 Corinthians 4:15. In Galatians 4:19 he
speaks of himself as having a mother's pangs for his children in the faith.

In chains. Onesimus was doubly dear to the apostle, being the child of
his sorrows.

12. I am sending him . . . back. The epistolary aorist is used for the present. It is clear both from the context here and from Colossians 4:7-9 that
Onesimus accompanied the letter.

Who is my very heart. A figure of speech common in all languages.

13. So that he could take your place in helping me. Compare

138

Philippians 2:30 and 1 Corinthians 16:17. With a delicate tact the apostle assumes that Philemon would have wished to perform these friendly offices in person if it had been possible.

In chains. An indirect appeal to his compassion (see verses 1, 9-10). In this instance, however, as in verse 9, the appeal assumes a tone of authority by reference to the occasion of Paul's bonds. For the genitive **for the gospel,** describing the origin, compare Colossians 1:23. They were not shackles which self had riveted but a chain with which Christ had invested him. Thus they were a badge of office or a decoration of honor.

14. But I did not want to do anything without your consent. In this verse **Any favor you do** is, "The benefit arising from you." That is, "the good which I should get from the continued presence of Onesimus and which would be owing to you."

15. He was separated from you. "He does not say," writes Chrysostom, "for this reason he fled, but, For this reason he was parted: for he would appease Philemon by a more euphemistic phrase. And again he does not say he parted himself, but, he was parted: since the purpose was not Onesimus' own to depart for this or that reason: just as Joseph also, when excusing his brethren, says (Genesis 45:5) 'God did not send me hither.'"

For a little while. "For an hour," "for a short season" (see 2 Corinthians 7:8; Galatians 2:5). "It was only a brief moment after all," the apostle would say, "compared with the magnitude of the work wrought in it. He departed a reprobate; he returns a saved man. He departed for a few months; he returns to be with you for all time and eternity!" This sense of **back for good** (Greek, "eternally") must not be arbitrarily limited. Since he left, Onesimus had obtained eternal life, and eternal life involves an eternal interchange of friendship. His services to his old master were no longer barred by the gates of death.

That you might have him back. In this context **have him back** may have one of two senses: first, "to have back, to have in return," or, second, "to have to the full, to have wholly," as in Philippians 4:18. In other words, the prominent idea in the word may be either "restitution" or "completeness." The former is the more probable sense here.

16. No longer as a slave. St. Paul does not say "slave" but **as a slave.** It was a matter of indifference whether he were outwardly a slave or outwardly free, since both are one in Christ (Colossians 3:11). But though he might remain a slave, he could no longer be **as** a slave. A change had taken place in him independent of his possible emancipation; in Christ he had become a brother. The **no longer as a slave** is an absolute fact, whether Philemon chose to recognize it or not.

As a man and as a brother in the Lord. "In both spheres alike, in the affairs of this world and in the affairs of the higher life." In the former, as

139

Meyer pointedly says, Philemon had the brother for a slave; in the latter he had the slave for a brother.

17. So if you consider me a partner. "If you hold me to be a comrade, an intimate friend." "Partners" have common interests, common feelings, common work.

> *18-22. If he has done you any wrong or owes you anything, charge it to me. I, Paul, am writing this with my own hand. I will pay it back—not to mention that you owe me your very self. I do wish, brother, that I may have some benefit from you in the Lord; refresh my heart in Christ. Confident of your obedience, I write to you, knowing that you will do even more than I ask. And one thing more: Prepare a guest room for me, because I hope to be restored to you in answer to your prayers.*

> *But if he has done you any injury or if he stands in your debt, set it down to my account. Here is my signature—Paul—in my own handwriting. Accept this as my bond. I will repay you. For I will not insist, as I might, that you are indebted to me for much more than this; that you owe me your own self. Yes, dear brother, let me receive from my son in the faith such a return as a father has a right to expect. Cheer and refresh my spirits in Christ. I have full confidence in your compliance as I write this, for I know that you will do even more than I ask. At the same time also prepare to receive me on a visit; for I hope that through your prayers I shall be set free and given to you once more.*

18. If he has done you any wrong. The case is stated hypothetically, but the words doubtless describe the actual offense of Onesimus. He had done his master some injury, probably had robbed him; and he had fled to escape punishment.

19. I, Paul. The introduction of his own name gives it the character of a formal and binding signature; compare 1 Corinthians 16:21; Colossians 4:18; 2 Thessalonians 3:17. A signature to a deed in ancient or medieval times would commonly take this form—"I—so and so."

This incidental mention of his signature, occurring where it does, shows that he wrote the whole letter with his own hand. This procedure is quite exceptional, just as the reason for the letter is exceptional. In all other cases he appears to have employed an amanuensis, only adding a few words in his own handwriting at the close.

Not to mention. "Not to say," as in 2 Corinthians 9:4. There is a suppressed thought: "though indeed you cannot fairly claim repayment," "though indeed you owe me as much as this."

Your very self. St. Paul was Philemon's spiritual father, who had given birth to him in the faith, and to whom therefore he owed his being.

20. Brother. This is the entreaty of a brother to a brother on behalf of a brother (see verse 16).

I. "I seem to be entreating for Onesimus; but I am pleading for myself; the favor will be done to me"; compare verse 17. The emphatic **I** identifies the cause of Onesimus with his own.

That I may have some benefit. "May I have satisfaction, find comfort in you"; that is, "may I receive such a return from you as a father has a right to expect from his child."

In the Lord. As he had given birth to Philemon **in the Lord** (compare 1 Corinthians 4:15, 17), so it was **in the Lord** that he looked for the recompense of filial offices.

21. You will do even more than I ask. What was the uppermost thought in the apostle's mind when he penned these words? Did he contemplate the emancipation of Onesimus? If so, the restraint which he imposes on himself is significant. Indeed, throughout this letter the idea would seem to be present in his mind, though the word never passes his lips. This reserve is eminently characteristic of the Gospel. Slavery is never directly attacked as such, but principles are inculcated which must prove fatal to it.

22. When St. Paul first contemplated visiting Rome, he had intended, after leaving the metropolis, to travel west to Spain (see Romans 15:24, 28). But by this time he appears to have altered his plans, wishing first to revisit Greece and Asia Minor. Thus in Philippians 2:24 he looks forward to seeing the Philippians shortly, while here he contemplates a visit to the churches of the Lycus valley.

There is a gentle compulsion in this mention of a personal visit to Colosse. The apostle would thus be able to see for himself that Philemon had not disappointed his expectations.

A guest room. "A lodging." The **guest room**, as a lodging, may denote either quarters in an inn or a room in a private house. In this case the response would doubtless be a hospitable reception in Philemon's home; but the request does not assume so much as this.

23-25. Epaphras, my fellow prisoner in Christ Jesus, sends you greetings. And so do Mark, Aristarchus, Demas and Luke, my fellow workers. The grace of the Lord Jesus Christ be with your spirit.

Epaphras, my fellow captive in Christ Jesus, greets you. As do also Mark, Aristarchus, Demas, and Luke, my fellow laborers. The grace of our Lord Jesus Christ be with you and your household and sanctify the spirit of you all.

23. Epaphras is mentioned first because he was a Colossian (Colossians 4:12) and, as the evangelist of Colosse, was doubtless well known to Philemon. Of the four others, Aristarchus and Mark belonged to the

Circumcision (Colossians 4:10-11), while Demas and Luke were Gentile Christians. All these were of Greek or Asiatic origin and would probably be well known to Philemon, at least by name. On the other hand, Jesus Justus, who is honorably mentioned in the Colossian letter (Colossians 4:11) but passed over here, may have been a Roman Christian.